THE ANGEL O

Books by Geert Mak

Amsterdam: A brief life of the city
Jorwerd / An Island in Time: The Biography of a Village
In Europe: Travels Through the Twentieth Century
The Bridge: A Journey Between Orient and Occident
In America. Travels with John Steinbeck

Geert Mak

The Angel of Amsterdam
Seven City Stories

Uitgeverij Atlas Contact
Amsterdam/Antwerpen

Original title *De engel van Amsterdam*
Original publisher Atlas Contact
Cover design Roald Triebels
Cover image Corbis / Monet
Author photo Merlijn Doomernik
Typography Perfect Service, Schoonhoven
Printer Koninklijke Wöhrmann, Zutphen

ISBN 978 90 450 2679 4
D/2014/0108/598
NUR 301

www.atlascontact.nl
www.geertmak.nl

For Mietsie

Contents

START

A city in blue

The predominant colours were grey, red and green, interrupted in the centre of town by the white of cornices and the brown of canals. Rusty streaks entered from left and right, with quick yellow lines on them. The area was completely encircled by ingeniously interlaced ribbons that bore slowly advancing chains of gleaming metal. All around was green, with beyond it the blue of infinite water. Shadows of clouds raced over the housing blocks of districts called South, East or Old West. In the narrow gardens fruit trees were blossoming, exuberant pink amid the grey.

In 1992 I flew above the city for the first time. There was a strong wind and we bobbed on the gusts, wave after wave, like a leaf on a turbulent lake. Below us Amsterdam lay like a safe, orderly, thriving, evenly breathing body.

The roof is often the first messenger – silent, subtle and unerring – to convey word of the lives beneath, and I'd seldom read so many tales of affluence, care and respectability as in the red pantiles, thick tar and coarse gravel below us. Red in North, reddish brown and white in South, grey and white in East, brownish grey in the city centre, and only in West, up against the central district, could I see, here and there, roofs with rust and rubbish, patches and blotches, like the hands of an elderly man.

The streets were remarkably quiet. On the southern outskirts I saw a newly built district, utterly still, white as a Kasbah, dusted with sand from a nearby building site. In North the land battled the water in an indeterminate region, part green, part grey, part bare earth, part everything that existed before it. In the distance were strips of dark-green trees and all the way to the horizon were shadows, moving steadily onwards, cloud after cloud. I saw a man walking a dog.

In the zoo strolled elephants and bears, big as young mice, and somewhere in the heart of the city a Star of David shone out, invisible from the earth. The old canals and quaysides were deserted, aside from a few pedestrians, like an eighteenth-century streetscape. The dead were sleeping, on this sunny and gusty day, beside avenues, flowerbeds and colonnades of trees, in thousands of greyish-white rectangles and blocks.

For a short time we followed the banner of a broad watercourse. To left and right ran the straight silver lines of drainage ditches. The green was solid and firm here, tucked up tight like a warm farmhouse bed. The air was full of voices. In South a house was being burgled. In West a shop robbed. In South-East someone was bleeding to death in the wreckage of a car. I saw the culprits running; I saw aid for the injured lose its way between the tower blocks.

The small gardens of South were waiting, with their pergolas and fancy white garden chairs, for the few hours of sun allotted them daily. I saw a square with four little girls skipping rope. Then we sailed on along the margins, past rusted ships and forgotten harbours, past docksides with thousands of shiny new cars, past long rows of big oil storage tanks and hidden hollows in the shrubbery where they still live, the fools and the prophets, in their shacks and shabby caravans.

Above the tall mirrored towers and concrete blocks of South-East, the sucking wind grabbed us. Far below were the birds, close to the roofs and the safety of trees. A swarm of starlings was all that slipped past in the depths. We flew back and approached the city once more, from the south-west on the back of a wind blast, a seagull racing alongside, somewhere half under us, tumbling over its wings. First came the white districts, then the greyish-brown, then the old man's hands, then a tower topped with a crown, the house fronts on the main belt of canals fashioned like small jewels, white window frames, glistening glass. And then, once again, the water.

Stone and earth on the Burgwal

I

I flew over Amsterdam one April afternoon behind the backs of pilot Willem van Donkelaar and observer-detective Léon Toen.

From the ground the PH-RPW police helicopter looks like a vicious beetle, a metal angel, a blue voyeur in the intimacy of the city, but inside the glass bubble there was a rather philosophical mood that afternoon as the two men performed their allotted tasks together, seeing the good and reporting the bad, then being forced to watch, powerless. 'This is Alex 82-19, Alex 82-19,' Alex in his thick flying suit told the control tower, but it sounded like 'Alex, caiperpetty, caiperpetty, Alex ack!' and we dropped down again, diagonally, in a gust of wind. We were off to look at a strange drum floating loose on the IJ, at what might be an illegal discharge, at a new settlement of indigents and refugees on a wild and desolate stretch of land, then at a suspiciously parked van. After that we just roamed for a while through the clouds above the city.

'Robbery on the Overtoom,' said Léon. Over the years he'd developed an eagle eye for hurrying figures and strangely bulging plastic bags. 'Bank left a moment, Willem, so I can get a better look. There, those two men there, stay with them...'

The world turned on its head and the city wheeled up along with it.

I saw the canalside streets almost empty, with only the occasional pedestrian. I could make out the Oude Kerk and the Nieuwe Kerk, the Burgwallen, the Dam, the Warmoesstraat, the Nieuwendijk, the bend in the Amstel. I saw more and more of the bird's-eye view that in 1538 Amsterdammer Cornelis Anthoniszoon saw in his imagination, the sea of houses he drew from above, along with the Waag on the Nieuwmarkt, the Schreierstoren, the Begijnhof, bridges, streets, main roads, roof profiles, old monastery complexes and, away beyond them at an almost hidden spot on one of the Burgwallen, the house in which now, more than four hundred and fifty years later, I'm writing these lines.

The house is near where the Damstraat becomes the Oude Hoogstraat and then the Nieuwe Hoogstraat. With its double front steps, its solid door and its heavy, broad cornice, it's the largest listed building on this narrow canal.

Around the corner the street is alive: bicycling schoolchildren, students with bags and binders, those two ever-cheerful girls at the flower stall, Amsterdam Hell's Angels, a clutch of American art historians, a punk girl, ladies from South who've come to buy Indian textiles, drunken tramps, excitable German women, sex tourists, urchins, pickpockets, construction workers and local officials – everyone and everything squeezes along the narrow thoroughfare, and where it goes to from here, no one knows.

But behind the old front door with its five locks, silence falls. There's a hall, a marble passage, a front house and a back annex, a complex of staircases where every newcomer gets lost; there are apartments, and attics rebuilt as 'lofts'; there's even an old chapel – now simply another apartment –

and, hidden away between the houses, a quiet old garden featuring a half-collapsed summer house with two pillars and no roof.

It's a typical dwelling, this house on the Burgwal, the city in a nutshell, a house that once smelled of punch and powder, of politics and trade, of love and madness, happiness and grief. The shadow of history has fallen over almost every aspect of it and much of the house will remain a mystery forever. Yet there are fragments, shards, a few lines of handwriting in an ancient deed, bits of a jigsaw that reveal something of the spirit that once prevailed in this accumulation of wood, brick and stone.

We found the first clues when we and the house were getting to know each other in the early 1980s, when a joint renovation moved through all its nooks and crannies like a storm. Behind the vaulting in the chapel we found remnants of hay and dung, as if it had once been some kind of stable, and up against the ceiling we could just make out a couple of faded old coats of arms. The big front room was still full of antique furniture, with handles crudely screwed on here and there as if someone had used it as a stable support in life. In a small side room, under many layers of paper, the walls were still covered with black chintz fabric. In garden sheds, beneath mud and chicken droppings, was a marble floor with a regular pattern of white squares. On an outside wall of the second floor we found, mystifyingly, the remains of a stepped gable, long since bricked over. In the darkly timbered attic was a strange wooden cage that looked like a bed in which someone could be shut up at night.

In a corner of a dormer window, builders had recorded their names during a long-ago lunch break: '*Hermanus Jan Schuurman, oud 18 jaar, gedaan den 1 junij 1871. Den 13 Oct 1891*' '*P.J.J. Inniger, Metselaar* [bricklayer], *14-12-1903*', '*P.J.S.*' and next to another window again: '*Hermanus Jan Schuurman, oud 18 jaar*'. We found textile samples, old hatboxes and a large trunk from Königsberg. There was a box full of envelopes and invoices and underneath them some bizarre correspondence between the Grasvelds – the last family to own the house – and a certain Goldberg, with wartime dates, an exchange of letters that smelled of persecution, disaster and possible treachery. And a bill from 1942: 'Expenses incurred for the care and burial of Franziska Michaëlis.'

Behind one of the beams, covered in dust, was a folder with drawings of black pine forests and menacing mountain views. Signed: Franziska Michaëlis.

Those were the first things the house revealed, and for some time they were all.

On paper practically nothing is left of the earliest years of the house, and the same goes for the city. The first mention of this part of the Low Countries dates from 12 October 1275, when Count Floris V gave 'the people who live at Amesteledamme' freedom from tollage for their trade goods. At that point almost a thousand people were living on two long, ribbon-shaped mounds on the banks of the mouth of the River Amstel, where it flows into the IJ. Their houses were on the Kerkstraat (now the Warmoesstraat), the Nes, the Wetering (today's Nieuwezijds Voorburgwal; the watercourse has since been filled in), the Kalverstraat and the Nieuwendijk, which was close to another small harbour on the Amstel. The

Dam was probably built across the river shortly before Floris v signed his act, to protect the hinterland from the rising waters of the IJ. Anyone today who crosses from the Ouderkerksplein to the Warmoesstraat or from Nieuwezijds Voorburgwal to the Nieuwendijk will notice that the road slopes upwards slightly. Those streets are all that remain of the paths that once led obliquely up onto the dyke behind which lurked the IJ – in those days still vast, blustery and brackish.

In its infancy the city must have looked like a Third World village, with houses made of wood, clay and reeds, no chimneys, pigs everywhere, the smell of fish, and a perpetual battle with water. The ground was soft, the houses kept sinking, and archaeological investigations indicate a repeated heaping up of the parcels of land. Centuries later, on the Nieuwendijk, more than four metres below street level, traces of some of the city's earliest inhabitants were found, including a fireplace (recognizable from the scorched Roman-style bricks), a few household effects and two ditches along the edges of the property. Its waste heap told the archaeologists most: thick layers of ash, a quantity of coal, scraps of iron and a few tools. There was everything to suggest that a family of blacksmiths had lived on that spot between about 1225 and 1275.

Other finds revealed that they were not the only specialist artisans to make their home on those low, narrow dykes. There was a foundry making castings in tin and brass, a shoemaker and tanner, a weaver and tailor, and a fishmonger. But otherwise this was a village of farmers and fishermen like any other. Seeds and micronutrients in the ground show that in those years the Amstel still had a wide fringe of reeds, dotted with ferns. Water plants grew in the river, wetland herbs on its banks. There were relatively few trees close to the Dam, but further upstream stood alder, in narrow bands along the river, accompanied by elder, hazel, guelder rose, red-flowering currant and honeysuckle. In some places old cereal grains recall the arable fields of many centuries past.

The pioneers did not live an isolated existence. On the plot inhabited by that first blacksmith, traces of silk were found – from Genoa, brought here via Bruges. Nonetheless, it was not until after 1300, when the city was given the right to hold a market near the Dam, that things really began to change. The farming and fishing families, who had previously done just about everything for themselves, started to outsource certain activities. From recovered millstones we can conclude that grain was milled by hand in the time of the city's early founders. The first windmill was built in 1307, on the Nieuwezijds Kolk, with a miller to work it. Bread was no longer baked on the floor of the hearth but by a baker in a proper oven. Among the first Amsterdammers whose names we know was one 'Lambrecht the baker', who by about 1310 was baking dough people had kneaded at home. Earthenware pots were no longer shaped entirely by hand but on a potter's wheel by someone who made it his specialty. New looms were introduced, more efficient but also more complicated, opening up opportunities for anyone who chose weaving as a vocation. The introduction of hops brought a better sort of beer, which was practically all anyone in the city drank in those days.

Trade developed, and money became an important factor in the economy. If a shoemaker in the village beside the Dam were to sell a pair of shoes in about 1250, he would not necessarily receive any money. He might be paid a few chickens, or a piece of salted pork. A hundred years later, money was the most normal thing in the world. People began to save; the first piggy banks found in Amsterdam date from around 1350. Trade was increasingly brisk. Freshwater fish like carp, eel, perch and pike had always been caught locally, but excavated bone fragments show that by about 1300 people were eating a lot of North Sea dab, plaice and flounder, and cod from Norway, supplied in dried form as 'stockfish'. Their herring came from southern Sweden.

In the second half of the fourteenth century, Amsterdammers began catching those species of fish themselves. Profits mounted. An ancestor of the Hoofts, for example, a family later famous for providing the city with burgomasters, was by origin a ship owner and ship's captain from Zaandam who, in his prime, appeared in The Sound as master of his own ship, thronged by seven other craft that belonged to him, each commanded by one of his seven sons. This was regarded as so extraordinary that the Danish king invited the whole family to dinner. It seems likely that from among those fish merchants, along with descendants of the original landowners, the first urban elite emerged.

That was how Amsterdam grew into a city over just a few decades in the fourteenth century, not by means of a Lord's charter and a list of formal privileges but by developing those features that have characterized all urban societies down through the ages: specialization and diversity.

Amsterdam urban archaeologist Jan Baart once compiled an inventory, based on discoveries at digs and a few early archival sources, of the trades practiced in fourteenth-century Amsterdam: blacksmith, cutler, goldsmith, crossbow-maker, coppersmith, tinsmith, shoemaker, tanner, sewer of bags and purses, belt-maker, turner, cooper, basket-maker, ship's carpenter, roofer, bricklayer, painter, sawyer, weaver, dyer, shearer, miller, oil-presser, baker, butcher, fishmonger, brewer, innkeeper, barber-surgeon, musician, prostitute, merchant, ship's captain, burgomaster, bailiff, alderman, clerk, steward, notary, schoolmaster, priest and anchoress.

Specialists relied on their craftsmanship and exclusivity, which made them more vulnerable than those who could turn their hands to anything. A basket-maker was able to earn a decent living only as long as ten other basket-makers did not come and settle in the same town. So with specialization came the problem of how to protect specialist groups – an issue that preoccupied the city throughout the centuries that followed.

The young city was soon protected against the surrounding countryside by privileges. Only within its walls could certain activities take place. Its various trades organized themselves into guilds, powerful lobby groups with strict admission requirements that every specialist was forced to join.

So the new settlement of Aemstelredamme quickly became a city, with all the concerns that accompany that status. On the Dam, tolls were levied on beer and a beer market developed, which brought farmers and fishermen living on the dyke into contact with traders from northern Germany and the Baltic. The Amstel became one of the most important approach routes to the inland waterways of Holland, which led on into the heart of Europe, and trade in grain and other bulk products bound for the south started up as well.

'Amsterdam has it' is today's slogan, and in a sense Amsterdam already had everything in the middle ages. It was unique in its time in connecting the northern Baltic trading routes with southern routes around Bruges, Ghent and Antwerp, and later even with Venice. The bulk transport of grain, beer and timber enabled specialization to develop on an international scale. The Baltic region concentrated increasingly on the cultivation of cereal crops, while in the Low Countries the stress came to be placed on craftsmanship, trade and other urban activities. Because large amounts of grain were imported, the growth of the urban population did not automatically lead to famine and impoverishment. In fact quite the opposite: as a result of specialization, prosperity grew.

Timber also arrived in great quantities, which allowed for the building of better, more competitive ships. The first fishermen on the IJ had fashioned their own boats from hollowed-out tree trunks, raising them a little with a couple of rough planks. Their grandchildren and great-grandchildren employed shipwrights to make far better if rather more complex craft, known as cogs and hulks. Centuries later, during the building of the Golden Tulip Hotel on the Oudezijds Kolk, the remains of the first large mediaeval shipyard were discovered: workshops, peat floors soaked with tar and caulk, and, right at the back, traces of a wooden structure more than thirty metres long, probably a rope walk. Further on, near the Lastage in what eventually became the Nieuwmarkt district, there must have been a constant hum of activity. Five hundred years later, remnants are still being found: shipbuilder's axes, coats of arms, gloves the craftsmen wore for their work, as well as discarded ship parts. Discoveries have included the oak rudder of a galleon in which Amsterdammers sailed the Baltic in about 1480.

Meanwhile, from 1300 onwards, the houses of the city were increasingly made of brick. In fact in 1400, after several major fires, the building of wooden houses was banned. Churches arose, beginning with the St Nicholas Church or Old Church (Oude Kerk). In the early 1400s a rich merchant called Willem Eggert gave up his orchard near the Dam for the building of a second church, St Catherine's or the New Church (Nieuwe Kerk).

The city's defences were improved. The first city wall ran inside the Oudezijds and Nieuwezijds Voorburgwallen – merely an earthen embankment with a wooden palisade on top and a narrow moat – but soon the young city burst its seams and after 1380 the land all the way to the Oudezijds Achterburgwal and the Nieuwezijds Achterburgwal was raised and made part of the city. A century later the process was repeated, this time extending Amsterdam as far as the Kloveniersburgwal and the Singel.

A solid, thick wall was then constructed around the city, with gates – the later Waag on the Nieuwmarkt started life as one of them – and bastions such as the Schreierstoren. Outside the wall was a bulwark, fortified at the far end by what later became the Montelbaanstoren. It was all aimed at defending the city against marauding bands of robbers from Gelderland, a countrywide menace in those years.

We know all this from ancient chronicles, from archaeological finds, from the few written records that have survived, the two mediaeval wooden houses still standing to this day and those few other buildings that have withstood time. But only the bird's-eye view painted by Cornelis Anthoniszoon, which now hangs in the Amsterdam Museum, opens up a window on the city as it was in reality, a snapshot of a clear, windy day in 1538. The pennants of the ships on the IJ stand stiff in the easterly breeze; we can see the city wall with the arches at its base, the rope walks on the Lastage, monastery orchards close to the wall, windmills, the lines that represent the Warmoesstraat, Kalverstraat and Zeedijk, and between them a sea of pointed gable ends, two or three storeys high, all in an area that stretched no further than the Munt and was no broader than the short walk from Oudemanshuispoort to the university library. Yet this was already, unmistakably, a city.

To the left, just inside the wall, in the shadow of a row of cloisters on the new stretch of land behind the defences, you can just make out the vague silhouette of the garden and house on the Burgwal, that scrap of brick, stone and earth at the heart of this brief history.

From the oldest records we know that the stretch of newly raised ground on the Burgwal was divided into building plots around 1500, and in the years that followed the district was gradually built on until it was full. Even before that, a monastery and a convent had appeared, the Minderbroedersklooster across from what is now the Waag, and next to the Sint-Jans Molenpad, beside the spot where the house on the Burgwal now stands, the Sint-Maria Magdalena in Bethaniënklooster. The latter, 'of the repentant sisters' as it came to be known, was originally intended for penitents who had placed themselves under a strict regime. It was not long, however, before women of the elite flocked in and the nunnery became a residence for ladies from the city's highest social circles.

A deed from 1472 has survived in which a garden is sold 'on the Zeedijk next to the repentant sisters' hay house' – reflecting the rural atmosphere of Amsterdam at the time. Only a small sluice separated the water in the canal from the wild, brackish IJ, and as tradition would have it, around 1550 a stray seal was spotted swimming in the water near the Burgwal. The embankment served as common land for grazing cows and horses, a stream ran through the Minderbroedersklooster (the Huidenvetterssloot, later filled in) and the sisters of the Bethaniënklooster specialized in fattening oxen (a street that later became known as the Koestraat passed through their convent). When the city wall was built across the back gardens of the houses and cloisters on the Achterburgwal in 1480, pigsties were immediately put up against it. On the map drawn by Cornelis Anthoniszoon, gardens are still visible, and between the Koestraat and the Barndesteeg is a courtyard with fruit trees.

It is hard to make out the house on the Burgwal in that first map by Cornelis Anthoniszoon. The building is small, lower than its neighbours. But on his second map, a woodcut made six years later, it is plainly in evidence, even if its precise shape is still not completely clear. Either the house had been altered considerably in the intervening years, or the mapmaker plotted the situation rather better the second time; we will never know for certain, and the archives tell us nothing.

In the cellars of the house we found huge, almost fossilised foundation beams, with notches suggesting they had previously been used to support a ceiling elsewhere. None of this tells us very much. It was probably a home like most others in those years, with an open 'front house', a fireplace and a closed inner hearth.

In early Amsterdam, dwellings consisted of little more

than a single open space, a large barn of sorts, with an open fire at the back from which smoke escaped through a hole in the roof. The back and front walls were made of wood and constructed in such a way that they could be pulled down quickly in case of fire – a great help to those fighting the blaze. A few buildings of this type probably still existed during the early years of our house. Until 1500 mention was made in city statutes of houses with a 'free hearth' or 'the fire you can go around', in contrast to the brick fireplaces and chimneys that came into fashion from the fifteenth century onwards. The disadvantage of those was that they drew more strongly, creating a draught, so some Amsterdammers started to construct a room around the fire by erecting partitions as draught-screens, which also helped to retain the warmth. This was a room that became known as the inner hearth, a place that for centuries would symbolize the intimate nature of Amsterdam's domestic culture. It was around the fireplace that everyone sat in winter to talk, to smoke, or simply to doze. The ceiling was often lowered, creating space for a separate room above, called the *insteek*, (literally: the insertion).

The 'front house' remained an extension of the street. It developed into the space familiar to us from paintings by Jan Steen and Johannes Vermeer: high, with a tiled floor, oblique light through a small leaded window, a front door that was usually open – apart from the lower section, to keep out wandering dogs – shutters that folded down and could be used to display wares, a table, a few chairs, a painting or two. In short, a half-private, half-public area that served as a shop, office and meeting place combined.

We know as little about the earliest residents of the house on the Burgwal as we do about the building itself. There are merely occasional clues. We have a rough idea what urban residents of the time ate: rye and barley bread, or, if they were particularly wealthy, 'court bread' or 'gentlemen's bread' made with wheat flour. Aside from that they lived on a diet of peas, beans, turnips, fish, poultry, hare, rabbit, cheese, butter, eggs, bacon, and gruel made with buckwheat, barley or oats. Vegetables and fruit were luxury extras. Bone fragments found during excavations show that more pork was eaten here than elsewhere in Holland, presumably because Amsterdammers had an unlimited right to let their pigs forage on the banks of the IJ.

The ordinary man seasoned his food with indigenous products such as salt, caraway, dill, chives, mustard and onions. But remains found here, even the oldest, include the seeds of raisins, currants and figs – evidence that the urban elite was familiar from the very start with products from far-off Italy and France.

As to what the inhabitants wore, we can draw certain conclusions from the earliest Amsterdam altarpieces and from paintings of civic guards. Amsterdammers, no matter how rich, usually went around in sober black, with just a small lace collar as decoration, the men wearing a kind of beret on their heads, the women a modest cap.

In 1978, close to the house on the Burgwal, a dredge pulled an item of leather clothing from the water of the Oudezijds Achterburgwal that with great care and attention to detail the experts were able to reconstruct. It turned out to be a sixteenth-century jerkin, with two panels at the front and two separately cut collars. The front fastenings made a strange impression. At the top, near the collar, were three cords, below them another two, followed by nothing at all, leaving the midriff section open, while at the bottom there was one more cord. The result was precisely the kind of jacket we see in paintings by Breughel, worn by merrily cavorting men with bulging bellies at peasant weddings or on other occasions that involved heavy drinking. This was originally the attire of the *Landsknecht* or mediaeval mercenary, but later, as these things often go, military dress was adopted by companies of civic guards and then by ordinary citizens who wished to appear brave and soldierly.

A few years ago, not far from the house, at the site of the shipyard on the Oudezijds Kolk, remnants of the household effects of an early sixteenth-century Amsterdam house were found. They present a detailed picture of the household of a well-to-do resident in those years: stackable tin cups, glass, pottery, the remains of a splendid Spanish majolica plate, an ornate dagger with a cow-bone handle and a wooden spinning top crowned with a silver coin. Amongst it all the archaeologists found several stones of a foreign and extremely rare fruit of which no trace had ever been found in previous excavations: the peach. Seemingly trivial, it was evidence of what must have been vast extravagance in this little town.

Of the earliest residents themselves – the bakers, fishmongers and merchants, or the proud women in those first civic portraits – nothing at all remains. Their graves were systematically cleared over the centuries, year after year.

Occasionally, during the building of an extension to a church for example, a forgotten grave dating from those earliest times is discovered: a rough coffin, a small corpse, a few jewels, committed to the earth at a time when the houses of the city were still made of wood and Miracle Processions still moved through the streets singing (or wailing, if famine or plague were abroad) with candles and banners, and children dressed as black devils, all suddenly exposed to the light amid the noise of pneumatic drills and the latest hit tunes of the modern city.

In the early 1990s the gravestones of the mediaeval St Olof's Chapel were lifted. I saw the coffins uncovered there, with dozens of skeletons of men, women, boys and girls, some with their heads to one side, others with their knees pulled up, sometimes the hands folded, sometimes not, some two to a grave, some alone, the babies and very young children close to the pulpit, the parents further away. The graves in the top layer were only a century old; beneath them lay rows of skulls and bones belonging to people of the eighteenth, then the seventeenth century, and the remains of jewellery and fans made of animal bone that were often buried with the richest of the women, whose bodies were beautifully laid out. Now all those people were jumbled together, and next to them stood a small yellow excavator that kept taking fresh mouthfuls of the bony ground to be carried off as rubble to a new housing estate on an island in the harbour in the eastern part of the city.

The first person named in the archives as the owner of the house was Clement Volckertszoon Coornhert. In a taxation listing from 1578 he is recorded as having three houses in his possession on this short stretch of the Burgwal. He had probably lived there since 1561. In an acknowledgement of debt dated 9 January 1561, he admits to owing money on a house in the Warmoesstraat and a house 'on the Oudezijds Achterburgwal, where he is currently living'.

Alterations were carried out at some point in those years, with the result that two houses became one. The archives say nothing on the subject, but the house speaks for itself. During the most recent bout of renovation, the ceiling in one of the large front rooms was removed and found to be hiding two sixteenth-century ceilings, with massive joists supporting the cross beams, that made it obvious two houses must have been combined. From the pattern of the broad, mediaeval floorboards beneath those ceilings you can still tell precisely where one house ended and the other began.

At that time Clement was in the prime of his life, a little over forty, and for years he had been among the richest of Amsterdam merchants. As one of the largest houses in town, this was a suitable dwelling for a man of his status. To this day its long walls run parallel to the canal, instead of perpendicular to it as in almost all other Amsterdam houses. That basic structure suggests that the original house was erected by someone who had ample materials and a great deal of money.

Clement's father, Volckert Janszoon Coornhert, was a highly respected cloth merchant who lived on the wealthy side of the Warmoesstraat, the side with the waters of the Amstel mouth at its back. His mother was from a rich Amsterdam family; her great-grandfather is recorded as being an alderman in 1430. His brother Dirck Volckertszoon Coornhert, several years younger, would later become a world-famous humanist and law reformer, but Clement was closer to his other brother, Frans, a notary and translator. The life of the Coornherts is illustrative of the spirit of independence that began to stir in the mid-sixteenth century, both in the house and in the still small city, with its fewer than ten thousand residents. In fact Clement's father, the cloth merchant, struck out on a path of his own in 1540, when he did something that must have seemed revolutionary in industrious, pre-Calvinist Amsterdam: at the height of a successful life he decided to stop working, declaring 'that he was rich enough', as his son Dirck later wrote. His wife, whose thinking on such matters was rather more old-fashioned, believed he ought to consider his children's future, but Volckert was of the opinion that they were perfectly capable of taking care of themselves, and anyhow he would prefer them to be 'honest and diligent earners' rather than 'idle and shameful consumers'. From then on, mother Coornhert ran the textile business, along with her daughter Katryn and her son Clement.

Shortly after Volckert's death, which was not long in coming, his son Dirck caused consternation in the family with a fresh bout of independent thinking. At nineteen he had travelled in Portugal and Spain, and on his return he was absolutely determined to marry Cornelia, a beautiful and kind but poor child of the common people. His mother refused permission, and with that Dirck lost his substantial inheritance. '*Verkiesen doet verliesen*' he wrote: 'choosing means losing'. He took a lowly job with Count Reynout van Brederode, whose household, and more besides, was managed by Cornelia's sister.

Dirck was truly artistic by nature, and it seems the city already had space for men of that sort. He translated large parts of *The Decameròn* and could play 'with great mastery' the 'German flute, as well as the lute and the harpsichord'. But what he did by marrying so far beneath him was extraordinary in the Amsterdam of his day. It seems rather like what his father had done, in that he was guided in the most important decision of his life not by religion, tradition or money but simply by his own personal feelings.

It was a genuine love match in sixteenth-century Amsterdam, and it lasted all their lives. Even the dry archival records that have come down to us are aglow with it: when Dirck is imprisoned in The Hague by the Spanish Duke of Alba's 'Council of Troubles' in 1567, Cornelia more or less deliberately allows herself to be infected with plague because she does not want to survive his execution; almost twenty years later, when Cornelia falls dangerously ill, Dirck breaks off the most important polemic of his career, a four-week debate with Leiden professor Adrianus Saravia, to go and nurse her; and when Cornelia's death finally puts an end to their life together, Dirck writes to his friend Hendrick Spiegel, in stiff but loving terms:

If beauty (as her Youth was), virtue (as her old age was) and kindness (as all her life was) may draw a man's heart to love, then it was right and fitting that my heart should love her. And so it indeed came to pass.

Clement initially adhered to all his mother's rigid traditions. Because his brother Dirck had decided to go his own way, Clement's inheritance was larger, which perhaps made it easier for him to finance the purchase and rebuilding of the house on the Burgwal. From old invoices we know that as late as 1549 he supplied red fabric to decorate the streets for the entry into Amsterdam of Emperor Charles V.

As the years went on, however, Clement and his brother Frans frequently found themselves in conflict with the ruling elite of the city, which was still strictly Catholic at this time. Frans settled in Naarden as a notary and Clement left for Vianen, but around 1560 he reappeared in the city, and on

25 May 1562 he was registered as a citizen again, a renowned cloth merchant, residing on the Oudezijds Achterburgwal. Frans also returned and we know that in 1558 he was appointed deputy bailiff. In 1565 the local magistrates tried to have Frans removed from his post as notary, but they were prevented from doing so. Higher authorities intervened.

Meanwhile, innumerable semi-clandestine meetings were held in the big, desirable residence on the Burgwal. Something was brewing in the city, and the brothers Frans and Clement Coornhert were starting to emerge as the most important leaders of the new and rebellious reformist movement. Their brother Dirck had set up an engraving studio in Haarlem, made his name as an amateur theologian and philosopher, worked his way up to the post of town clerk and was now advancing to become one of the most important diplomats and advisors to William of Orange and the new Dutch Republic.

We should be careful not to romanticize the rebel movement that arose in the city and elsewhere in the Low Countries. In a place like Amsterdam, the concepts 'Catholic', 'Lutheran', 'Baptist' or 'Calvinist' were often simply an indication of the family clan to which you belonged. In some respects Amsterdam's battle between the Catholics and the new denominations – part of a conflict that arose all over Europe at that watershed moment in the middle ages – was little more than a struggle between old and new urban elites.

Yet there was more to it than that. The independent behaviour of father Volckert and son Dirck Coornhert reflected a different mentality, one that was slowly starting to take possession of the city.

As early as 1452, Philip the Good, Duke of Burgundy, called Amsterdam the greatest mercantile city in Holland, and when several years later it leapt at the chance to buy from Emperor Maximilian the right to depict the imperial crown on all its ships (a major public relations coup in the mediaeval world), the young trading centre established its name internationally. The pride and self-confidence of its residents grew.

Those feelings were boosted by the fact that this low-lying, sodden city, like all of Holland, had been wrested from the water by her citizens with their own hands and they were forced to do battle with that inherited common enemy time and again. The residents of the young city needed to organize themselves and their government efficiently from the start, and to avoid making too much of every argument. Preparing each stretch of new land for building must have been an unimaginably arduous task, involving more work than construction itself. Within just a few years, hundreds of manual labourers were being called upon to slice out, load and transport many tens of thousands of cubic metres of clay and lay it down on the watery peat. The municipal authorities gained great expertise in tackling large-scale public works, and all that activity gave the people of the city a natural sense of citizenship: this bit of the world was wholly the fruit of their labours.

Amsterdam gained in self-confidence. Towards the end of the middle ages, cities all across Europe grew increasingly powerful. They were the bastions of those autonomous citizens who were gradually taking the place of the weakened and impoverished aristocracy. The Low Countries, which had far too little agricultural land to keep everyone in work, took the lead in this sense. By 1514 more than half the people of

Holland lived in cities. Amsterdam, where the residents had always done everything themselves and the aristocracy never made any headway, anticipated this trend, and ascendant Calvinism, with its doctrine of virtue and grace, provided a religious framework that perfectly suited the mentality of the hardworking, increasingly profitable mercantile city and its free-thinking entrepreneurs. They were the 'chosen people', who with 'God's strength' would divide the waters of the Red Sea and be led out from under 'Pharaoh's yoke' to the 'promised land of Canaan'.

When the Habsburg emperor Charles V died and left his realm to his son Philip II, it was inevitable, in retrospect, that conflict would arise. The empire's centre of gravity instantly moved south, to Philip's ascetic, sombre study in the Escorial. Amsterdam, along with the rest of the Low Countries, suddenly found itself on the periphery of an empire ruled with grim rigour, demoted from a centre of trade to something resembling a colony.

All kinds of extra taxes were introduced, foreign soldiers traversed the land and non-Catholics were harshly persecuted. Philip had the formal right to do all these things but they no longer reflected the actual balance of power. Everywhere in the Low Countries resistance grew, with William of Orange, as is often the case with great leaders, initially in the role of mediator and only later that of chieftain and figurehead.

An unexpected escalation of the smouldering conflict prompted the Amsterdam Coornherts to step forward. They became official spokesmen for what was called the *Gereformeerde Gemeente*, the Reformed Congregation. It put Dirck in an awkward position once again in relation to his family, this time because of his role as a diplomat for William of Orange.

On 23 August 1566, heralded by rumours reaching Amsterdam from other cities, trouble flared. A large crowd moved along the Burgwallen on both sides of the city, shouting and clamouring, and the monasteries and convents were targeted one by one. A storm of iconoclasm raged through the Oude Kerk. The hated Minderbroedersklooster, headquarters of the war on heresy, was besieged. The magistrates stood, heads bowed, on the steps of the house on the Burgwal to ask whether the Coornhert brothers might perhaps speak to the people, who were rampaging a few blocks further along the canal, and begged them to try to forestall the imminent storming of the monastery. They did so, but their mediation was brief.

In February 1567, Frans Coornhert decided to join the rebel movement, the Sea Beggars. We know from the archives that along with Laurens Jacobsen Reael – after whom today's Realengracht is named – he travelled to Vianen, where he consulted Hendrik, Lord of Brederode (nicknamed 'the Great Beggar'). Their talks were ostensibly about business matters, since there were reports of a quarrel between Clement and Hendrik over a brewery. Frans then moved on to Antwerp, where the Prince of Orange resided, to ask his advice. In April he was back.

Meanwhile Clement Coornhert had smuggled the Lord of Brederode into Amsterdam to prepare the city's surrender. Under pressure from a large crowd that gathered on the Dam, the municipal authorities were forced to appoint Brederode 'Captain-General', which in effect meant he assumed military command of the city.

Lord Heinderik Captainderik, as Brederode soon came to

be called, took rooms at an inn on the Dam, 'with Samson on its sign', and from contemporary reports – this troublemaker was naturally kept under close surveillance – it seems the Coornhert brothers would regularly walk along the Oude Hoogstraat in the evenings to drink a glass of beer with Brederode and his pal Treslong, and to play for a while on the 'game board' (probably a kind of backgammon).

Not long before this, their brother Dirck, the diplomat, had been saddled with a particularly difficult task by William of Orange. Amsterdam's Reformed Congregation had not in the end looted the Minderbroedersklooster, but they had taken over the chapel for their own services of worship. At this stage in the revolt, William of Orange did not want to provoke his country's Spanish governor-general Margaret of Parma any further, so he asked the Reformed to vacate the chapel. Dirck Coornhert was responsible for conveying the message, which meant he had to act against his own brother Clement.

Just what personal relations between the two brothers were like is unclear. Their loyalty to each other was probably quite strong, but then there was always that family trouble surrounding Dirck's marriage. In these turbulent times the divide between them became visible again, if in a rather different way. By marrying Cornelia, Dirck had put personal love above the traditionalist demands of his mother. Now he gave every individual's own religious experience a central role in his writings, placing it above the directives of any established church, whether Catholic or Calvinist. His brothers Clement and Frans, by contrast, adhered to the line taken by the Beggars, who wanted to make the city a theocracy, its people ruled by God and the Calvinist clergy.

In other words, Dirck opted for a personal form of religion, with an inner voice as its sole oracle, and in his later writings he fulminated with increasing passion against the persecution of heretics, be they Catholic or Protestant. Both sides therefore had him in their sights: Alba's bloodhounds were permanently at his heels, but in later years it was only the protection of William of Orange and his successor Maurice of Nassau that prevented the Calvinists from going after him as well.

In the city of Amsterdam, Clement was victorious for years, Dirck for centuries.

In late April 1567 came word that the Duke of Alba was on his way with a large army to put down the Dutch Revolt. William of Orange fled, Brederode left town and things grew too hot even for the Coornhert brothers. Their entire faction departed, along with many other dissidents, for the town of Emden in northern Germany, which was governed by Lutherans and the Reformed. They stayed there for several years, and when they returned after the Alteration – when Amsterdam switched sides to join the Protestant faith – Clement's house on the Burgwal grew to become one of the city's most important centres of support for the Prince of Orange.

Meanwhile, during the absence of the Coornhert brothers, terrible and miraculous events occurred around the house and elsewhere in the city. Both the Beggars and Alba's troops ranged back and forth across the country, looting and burning. There was famine in Amsterdam. People lay dead in the streets. 'They rotted there as if they were the carcasses of animals, and were eaten by the dogs and the birds,' wrote an Amsterdam priest, Father Wouter Jacobszoon, in his journal. He tells of the miracles that took place in the city: a young mother was found frozen to death on a dyke, but she still had milk in her breast, and her baby was alive and suckling.

Wouter Jacobszoon describes watching the funeral procession of a Spanish officer as it crossed the Dam and made its way along the Burgwal to the Minderbroedersklooster. The coffin was carried by four of the monks, each of them holding a wax candle, and by four Spaniards, 'and ahead of the corpse walked the entire monastery of Minderbroeders, some forty in number, with a cross at the front, and behind the corpse followed the pastor of the Nieuwe Kerk, with six or seven priests'.

These were the final tableaux of mediaeval Amsterdam. The city would always remain Catholic to some extent, behind a semblance of established Calvinism, and soon a blind eye was being turned to secret Catholic gatherings, but the hegemony of the Church of Rome was over. The priority for this increasingly important mercantile city with its diverse population was peace and order, a climate in which to do business. That was incompatible with the oppression of people who had come from abroad or who deviated from the accepted way of thinking.

One afternoon, almost by chance, I came upon a remarkable document in the Amsterdam City Archives. In a footnote I had found a reference to a dusty mayoral dossier that was said to contain something written by Clement Coornhert. This time the people at the desk needed to put in a good deal of effort. Phone calls were made, microfiches searched, computer files examined. Then, after half an hour, a lift came down, a door swished open, a brownish-yellow folder appeared and suddenly I was holding a letter written on 19 December 1576, sent from Delft by one Clement Coornhert.

He wrote: 'May you set an example to the poor who are dear to you, within and without. See also the wondrous deeds of the Lord that He hath wrought in these matters.'

The letter was addressed to Berend Claeszoon, 'In the Three Angels', beside The Water, and it was in fact a call to rebellion. In elegant pen strokes, Clement reported that the States, in the name of the Prince of Orange, had sent a drummer to Amsterdam to ask the city to transfer its allegiance to the camp of the Beggars, in order to 'drive out the foreign barbarism of the Spanish and be delivered', so that 'the good fatherland may return to its old cheer'. Berend Claeszoon was asked to pass the letter on to 'good friends who do hold you dear' and to 'help by the best means whatever is possible, that well-being may be advanced'.

The fact that this subversive letter ultimately ended up with the burgomasters is disconcerting, and no one any longer knows what happened to that brave drummer and his mission. It is one of many forgotten dramas in the history of Amsterdam. The letter is all that remains, with its small seal, and the folds that Clement made in the paper on that far off nineteenth of December, as if they were made only last week.

I will try one more time to imagine the house on the Burgwal as it must have been in those early years. Later the city would fill up like a rat's nest, but at first life remained quiet and peaceful on the canal. There were houses, but there were also long, overgrown walls with secluded gardens behind them, and orchards. Immediately beyond, the countryside began. A view of the city in profile from 1547 shows the green of spacious gardens behind the house. It must have smelled of apples there in autumn, and in summer of hay.

The interior will have been sober. In the sixteenth century even the richest Amsterdam merchants lived modestly. No doubt religious paintings were on display, along with portraits of the master and mistress of the house, and perhaps a few maps, but that would be all. With the exception of a few silver cups and spoons, there was hardly anything made of gold or silver. People like the Coornherts ate out of tin and earthenware.

The portraits of those first owners lie buried somewhere under the four centuries that separate them from us. We do know what Dirck Coornhert looked like: bearded, with a blunt, square face. And in 1566 a police spy recognized Frans at a secret meeting by 'his coarse speech'. We know nothing about Clement, but to judge by the civic guard portraits in the museum he will have worn the same dark, sober clothing as all the other merchants, with a kind of French beret on his head, his appearance enlivened at best by a chain or a ring.

Yet even for those black-clad merchants, change was on its way, and inside them they carried all the seeds of the great cultural and commercial explosion that would shake the city to its foundations less than a quarter of a century later, in the period that has gone down in history as the Dutch Golden Age. The Coornherts were not just merchants and politicians. In their own small way they exemplified the ideal Renaissance citizen, *homo universalis*, who had the highest aspirations imaginable in work, in politics and in the fine arts.

The house on the Burgwal must have seen a great deal of political activity, but there will also have been dancing, music, and singing to the accompaniment of the still relatively unmetrical, psalm-style music that was then in fashion. The city was small enough for its residents to know every street, and its art-loving ladies and gentlemen were a select and cheerful bunch. The Coornherts were part of that circle, as were the poet Pieter Janszoon Spieghel and old Cornelis Pieterszoon Hooft. Frans Coornhert was a poet himself and the archives show that he was a member of a chamber of rhetoric called Uit Levender Jonst. Spieghel dedicated the following poem to Clement:

On Coornhart's Use and Abuse of Worldly Goods
Which is rich and mild, revealed here we find
Full candles of knowledge, that openly illuminate
Corn, wine and food, to bolster the mind
Cordially shared so that all may partake

In 1594, when Frans was seventy-five, he took part in a tableau vivant on the occasion of Prince Maurice's visit to the city. It depicted David's victory over Saul, and to the audience it could not have been plainer who was David and who was Saul, or on which of them God had conferred his blessings. Frans Coornhert was Saul.

He died in 1605, having reached an advanced age, but by then times had changed. The house had a new master, and Saul's days were over.

2

There is a map dating from 1625 that shows, in the heart of the city, on the Dam, something rather strange: three concentric circles, the largest of which would be about fifteen metres in diameter on the ground. In a later print of the map they have gone, as has the little old town hall, replaced by the substantial palace that stands there to this day.

Those circles were a fading remnant of mediaeval Amsterdam. They once functioned as part of a procedure in which a person was stripped of his citizenship, an almost magical ritual that took place around the city's navel. If debts owed by a citizen of the old city rose beyond a certain level, then in the final phase of bankruptcy proceedings he would be led three times around the circles – originally around the city itself – and anyone willing to stand surety for him was asked to make himself known. Only after that could a citizen be expelled from the community and imprisoned for debt.

On that same map, not a hundred metres away, is the house on the Burgwal, and if we look through a magnifying glass we can see that it has changed considerably. It now has three stepped gables, after the latest fashion, one at the front and two at the sides. That energetic merchant Pelgrom van Dronckelaer must have become its owner in about 1600. In 1603 he bought the smaller house next door from the widow of surgeon Cornelis Roos. It stretched from the Burgwal as far back as the kitchen of his own house. During our renovation work almost four centuries later, we came upon the remains of that kitchen, more than four metres under the floor of the large room that was eventually built over it: flagstones and old tiled walls, the hue of the tiles continually shifting in daylight, from light grey or beige to a sublimely delicate pink. That strange stepped gable bricked into the side wall on the second floor suddenly takes on a new significance as well; it is the same gable that you can find – if you look closely enough – on the 1625 map, sticking up above the north side of the house that belonged to Pelgrom van Dronckelaer.

Van Dronckelaer was a wealthy man. Among other things he was a governor of the Home for Elderly Men and Women, an underwriter – we know he insured the first ships ever to sail to the Cape of Good Hope – paymaster to the municipal soldiery and collector of payments for the lottery in Haarlem. On this corner of the Burgwal he steadily expanded his property portfolio, house by house, until he owned a complex of dwellings and warehouses that was impressive for its time. His family and their relatives by marriage lived there for over a century. On the 1625 map it is all clearly visible: the house on the Burgwal and three or four houses on the side street, their rear exits all giving onto a shared inner courtyard. There is a wall, then a patch of green between the houses, including something that looks like a vegetable plot. An unusually long outbuilding from Pelgrom van Dronckelaer's time still stands in the garden, up against the neighbouring houses, a grubby structure with a marble floor. It was probably a gallery once, a covered space open on one side such as were quite often built along the edges of courtyards in the seventeenth century.

Pelgrom van Dronckelaer was originally from Amersfoort, and there were many like him, thousands upon thousands of newcomers who caused the city to burst out of its walls in the late sixteenth century. After the fall of its main rival Antwerp in 1585, Amsterdam's economic expansion gathered pace. Countless 'Spanish Brabanters' (to use the name given to one such immigrant from the Southern Netherlands by Bredero in his most famous play) fled north and the number of residents quickly rose from thirty thousand to more than a hundred thousand. They included many merchants, who further increased the dynamism of the new city with their southern verve. But a committee of inquiry set up by the governors concluded that most newcomers were ordinary poor devils who were often forced to live by begging, and who tended to settle outside the city in 'humble little dwellings' or in hovels built up against the city wall, sometimes even niches in the wall itself.

At the point when Pelgrom van Dronckelaer moved into the house, Amsterdam was barely any bigger in surface area than a century before, even though it had more than five times as many inhabitants. This inevitably had a drastic effect on the social climate. The best possible use was made of every bit of space and the map by Cornelis Anthoniszoon shows quite a few tall houses, some with as many as three or four storeys. That upward development continued for centuries. A roof would be raised and one or more floors simply 'slid' underneath it, as long as the foundations could take the weight. All the land in between was eventually used to build alleys and passageways. Plots belonging to monasteries and convents were subsumed. Soon the garden behind the house on the Burgwal was the only patch of green in the area, and so it would always remain.

A map by Pieter Bast dated 1597 indicates just how full the city was by then. The house on the Burgwal is hemmed in by two tall neighbouring buildings on the canal and a huge dwelling on the Bethaniënstraat, apparently made of wood, that seems to extend behind the canalside house, forming an annex to it. There is only a little green space left at the back and all the trees have gone.

The hustle and bustle in the streets, the stench and filth created by all those people living in such a small area must have been astonishing, as dusty statutes and ordinances in the archives testify: bans on the emptying of chamber pots onto the street from upstairs windows; bans on the dumping of refuse, on letting pigs wander freely, on having front steps or signboards in narrow streets.

Only after Amsterdam switched sides to join the Beggars and a new, Calvinist patrician clan came to power, could serious work begin on a fresh expansion of the city. First of all, three islands were built in the IJ – a method by which the townsfolk outwitted the land speculators. The islands were named Uilenburg, Rapenburg and Marken, and they were the start of what would later become the Nieuwmarkt neighbourhood. Houses were built on them, although plenty of space was left for wharves and warehouses. This became a district for newcomers, especially Jews who had fled Spain, as did a fourth island, Vloonburg, land reclaimed from the Amstel that would later become the Waterlooplein.

On the other side of town the defensive wall was replaced by a modern system of earthen embankments and ramparts, and at the same time a new skin was added to the city, about a hundred and fifty metres wide. The original outer moat, the Singel, was promoted to the status of residential canal. Further out came houses and a street, then the embankment and beyond that a new canal that would eventually be called the Herengracht. By about 1586 the entire project was complete.

But the city's population kept on growing, and barely twenty years later the decision was made to expand even further. This third enlargement introduced the beginnings of Amsterdam's famous crescent-shaped 'belt' of canals. It was an audacious project: the Herengracht was widened, around it came a third canal, the Keizersgracht, around that was a fourth, the rather more downmarket Prinsengracht, outside of which a large district was built to house tradesmen and labourers called, for reasons that have never been fully explained, the Jordaan ('jardin'? 'the promised land across the Jordan'?), and beyond that, finally, on what are now the Nassaukade and the Stadhouderskade, an embankment and fortification such as befitted a city as rich as Amsterdam. The canals were intended for wealthy residents, of whom the city now had so many, and they were generous in design. Behind each house was ample space for gardens and greenery, and noisy or dirty commercial operations were forbidden. In the same period, a further two large island complexes were constructed on land reclaimed from the IJ, where people could both live and work: the Prinseneiland to the west and Wittenburg and Kattenburg to the east.

Within a few decades Amsterdam had been transformed. Anyone with money could escape the cramped inner city and have a spacious new house built for them on the Herengracht or the Keizersgracht. It therefore seems remarkable that it took so long for much of the urban elite to move to the new canals.

Pelgrom van Dronckelaer was buried in the Oude Kerk on 1 September 1620, his daughters Margriet and Geertruyt married a burgomaster and a future high sheriff respectively, but all his children continued to live in the complex on the Burgwal. Only his son Casper eventually made the move to the Herengracht, and that was only much later, after he married.

This attitude was typical of many Amsterdam notables. The city's elite has always avoided pomp and circumstance and fashionable excesses, a few exceptions aside. The richest woman in eighteenth-century Amsterdam, for example, the widow Pels on the Herengracht, had a fortune of two million guilders and a staff of five servants. The facade of her house remained relatively sober, and although there were some signs of wealth inside, the real money was kept in the bank, in the form of investments for the present and future. So in Amsterdam a townscape emerged that remained largely untouched by the Renaissance, the Baroque, the grandeur of absolutism and the major urban restructuring typical of the nineteenth century. Even the proud Amsterdam of the Golden Age was the opposite of a modern city by the European norms of its day: traditional and geared to individual citizens rather than a powerful aristocracy. For centuries the standard Amsterdam dwelling had essentially the same floor plan as a mediaeval town house.

Making money was one thing at which those Amsterdam merchants truly excelled. Every time the city expanded, a great deal of speculative investment took place, first of all by families that had played a part in municipal government and were therefore the first to hear of new plans. One of the burgomasters, Frans Oetgens, invested heavily in parcels of land near the Haarlemmerpoort in about 1609, which he was then able to sell to the city at a considerable profit.

The Van Dronckelaer family was not averse to such activities either. How Geertruyt van Dronckelaer's husband, Jan ten Grootenhuys, secured the post of high sheriff is a story in itself, but that he made good money out of it is beyond question. Among other things he was involved, in his role as a judge, in legal proceedings concerning permission to build what later became the Ronde Lutherse Kerk, and according to the Lutherans themselves he did a good job of propitiating the other judges with banquets and gifts. His brother-in-law Cornelis van Dronckelaer was a merchant, an alderman, a captain of the civic guard and a church warden at the Nieuwe Kerk, while Casper van Dronckelaer was a church warden at the Oude Kerk and, along with his colleagues, had a firm grip on the reins as far as pew rent, for example, was concerned.

This way of governing the city remained customary for centuries, yet objections to it were quite often raised. In 1640, shortly before the all-important Feast of St Nicholas (Sinta Klaas) on the fifth of December, a number of bookshops were found to be selling the defamatory pamphlet 'Sint-Nicolaes milde gaven, aen d'Amstelse jonckheyt' (The mild gifts of St Nicholas to the youth of Amsterdam). In this lampoon in verse, the saint was depicted as sitting on a chimney stack looking out over the city and calling to mind all the machinations and scandals of the past year, just as Sinta Klaas would traditionally recall the sins and virtues of children.

When sheriff Jan ten Grootenhuys and his aldermen heard about the pamphlet they exploded with rage, in the first instance, presumably, because it made a laughing stock of their families. All the copies the sheriff's men could get their hands on were confiscated, and on St Nicholas Day itself, three booksellers were arrested and interrogated by Jan ten Grootenhuys. Fresh arrests followed, including those of several famous city poets, publishers and gossipmongers.

What was it that agitated Jan ten Grootenhuys so much, less than a century after the religious debates of the Coornherts?

In the University Library, in the Rare and Valuable Works department, I asked to look at the pamphlet, and sure enough there it was. The slanderous text that no one was allowed to read has been carefully preserved down through the centuries.

The subtitle reads 'Ofte het laetste Quartier der Amsterdamsche Mane-schijn' (Or the last quarter of the Amsterdam Moonshine). The ancient paper is brittle. 'Oh, that in my great old age I should live to see such a wretched and corrupt state,' the anonymous poet has Sinta Klaas sigh on his chimney on the first page of the pamphlet, but then he lets fly staunchly enough, and he seems well-informed about the world of the fashionable and rich young people of his day.

Everyone drinks, smokes 'stinking tobacco', wallows in the 'new Spanish juice' and wears clothes 'after the fashion of the Court'. One of the sons of notables is compared to a beautiful but large building, always cold and dark. Another son is said to call the maid up to the attic 'with two balls out of his pants'. A third, a burgomaster's son, attends church piously enough but gets up to all kinds of things on the sly. Another is 'such a hot cat that he caterwauls in everyone's house. For he'll even jump over water if he knows of a pretty puss.'

Precisely what it was that inspired Jan ten Grootenhuys personally to go after heretics becomes apparent after a few pages and it seems it had to do with none other than his son Pelgrom ten Grootenhuys, who is introduced by name:

Pelgrom will now learn his lesson
And soon be a distinguished figure
For he knows how to manage his pennies
And he too will fill his ledger.

Then the boy's relationship with his girlfriends is addressed: 'Since he keeps that sweet little girl / For his daily breakfast'.

Another dig is probably intended for Pelgrom's nineteen-year-old brother Joan, who walks up and down the Warmoesstraat all day for some 'little dove' or other. The passage ends with the verse:

Greatness torments you, sweet coz
And so dominates the mood
That he thinks: there is no split
That does not desire his mug.

Pelgrom ten Grootenhuys would later marry a certain Elisabeth van Duynen and for the rest of his life he resided in one of the buildings in the complex on the Bethaniënstraat. Joan became a rich merchant. He moved in with his uncle Cornelis to live at the large house on the Burgwal and inherited it after Cornelis died. At the age of about fifty his fortune was estimated at a hundred thousand guilders, making him one of the hundred richest men in the city, a multimillionaire by today's standards.

For Amsterdam too, these were the best of times. Its dissidents included citizens who were far from lowly, and thousands of accomplished merchants, scholars, artists and craftsmen had arrived in Amsterdam fleeing religious persecution in their native France, Spain or the Southern Netherlands. Here, suddenly, everything was possible and anything went.

The increasing vivacity of Amsterdam can be seen in the portraits commissioned by companies of civic guards (the citizens' militia) in the years that followed. The dark clothing of the sixteenth century has given way to bright and multicoloured garb; the small collars and modest berets have grown into huge ruffs and brims, and the company of civic guards commanded by Captain Cornelis van Dronckelaer in 1626 clearly delighted in its own colourful elegance. Immigrants from Antwerp, Portuguese Jews who had fled Spain and later the Huguenots from France, along with the original residents of the city, generated a whirlwind of activity in a metropolis that must have had the same power of attraction in those days as New York has in our own.

There are all kinds of economic factors that explain the flourishing of the city in the seventeenth century, but at least as important as any of them was the psychological climate. Amsterdam had the dynamism of a place full of outsiders, people who had shaken off the middle ages. They were profoundly attached to their new city, but they maintained links with countless European towns and villages through a network of thousands of invisible threads spun out of letters, thoughts and dreams.

It made Amsterdam cosmopolitan, a quality it has never completely lost in all the years since, and in that respect the Jews were essential. To persecuted scholars like Descartes and Spinoza, the city was a peaceful oasis where intellectual ideas from all over Europe could be freely printed and sold. For the merchants an exchange bank was introduced – unique in Europe – and the beginnings of a fully-fledged banking system. The fine arts were extraordinarily popular. Paintings were sold at street markets and every house had a picture on the wall. On the Breestraat, not far from the house on the Burgwal, Rembrandt van Rijn from Leiden started a small painting factory, and in the lively, almost orientally busy 'Jewish' Breestraat he had no shortage of models for his biblical scenes. A little further away two large new synagogues were built, one for the 'German' Ashkenazim and one for the 'Portuguese' Sephardim. When they were consecrated, the promise of this 'Jerusalem of the West' was set down on a memorial stone for future centuries: 'This house of worship dedicated to God fears no coercion of conscience, nor torture or death...'

Dutch trading expeditions, departing from Amsterdam, travelled all over the world. In 1595 the first ships sailed to the East Indies – of the two hundred and forty-nine men who set out, only eighty-seven saw the city again two years later – and in 1609 members of an Amsterdam expedition were the first Europeans to lay eyes on a tree-covered island in the far west, full of birds and the scents of flowers – today's Manhattan.

A contemporary painting of the Dam depicts the people of Amsterdam: merchants from all points of the compass (several of them even wearing large, oriental turbans), bargemen, dockworkers, saleswomen, prominent personages and beggars. By 1650 the number of residents had risen to some two hundred thousand.

The city changed, and inside the house on the Burgwal the atmosphere must have slowly changed along with it. The pattern of meals was adjusted. In the Coornherts' household there were probably only two meals a day, the midday dinner at eleven in the morning and a small repast in the evening. But under the influence of trade, which required more time in the mornings, the city's main meal shifted further and further towards noon, along with trading times on the stock exchange. So the need arose for a small meal earlier in the morning, and the young Pelgrom ten Grootenhuys will almost certainly have breakfasted on bread, meat, smelt (a small fish) and a glass of beer.

The language spoken in the house changed radically as

well. Among themselves the Coornherts probably spoke the old Amsterdam dialect, which must have been more like present-day Afrikaans than modern Dutch, but under the overwhelming influence of all those immigrants the language vanished from the face of the earth. Even by Pelgrom van Dronckelaer's time a third of the people of the city spoke a broad Antwerp dialect and its most well-to-do citizens French. No one who aspired to be somebody would venture a word in the coarse tongue of Holland.

By studying the work of Bredero, that famous writer of early seventeenth-century farces, and certain dialects from the district around Zaandam, it has proved possible to reconstruct a little of the original Amsterdam language – especially the swear words, since in that crowded city cursing was something at which people excelled. This is roughly what must have been heard among servants at the back of the house, or indeed anywhere else: *'Gy hoer, gy slet-vinck!' 'Gy meervarcken, wout-aep, wout-esel, lelijcke pry!' 'Gy karoonje, gy vel met een gat!'* A literal translation captures the gist: 'You whore, you slut-finch!' 'You sea-hog, jungle-ape, jungle-ass, ugly leek!' 'You carcass, you skin with a hole!'

Towards the end of the seventeenth century, the house on the Burgwal was given a new name: De Schaep (The Sheep). But as for the city being the seventeenth-century equivalent of New York, that was over. Its role on the world market increasingly passed to others after 1650, the English in particular. In the house the dynasty of the Van Dronckelaers had ended. Cornelis died in 1659, Caspar in 1666, their nephew Joan in 1679. His children, Jan and Geertruyt, remained in residence.

Geertruyt, who was extremely rich and now approaching thirty, was courted soon after her father's death. On 1 October 1680 she married a younger man, Jan Fontijn Janszoon, who moved into the big house with her and changed his name to Jean de la Fontaine.

What exactly happened after that cannot be reconstructed from the archives, but things did not go well. There seems to have been a family row about the little dwellings on the Bethaniënstraat. Behind the house, on the site of the old outdoor kitchen, a stable was built, and spending continued at a great rate after that, despite the fact that all across the city fortunes were rapidly declining.

After twelve years, Jan Fontijn and Jan ten Grootenhuys were declared bankrupt. Their share of the house was sold. Geertruyt was not included in the bankruptcy proceedings and she relinquished her part of the house only after another eight years, on 9 October 1700. By then she was fifty. How fortune treated her in her impoverished old age we cannot tell. She lived for another twenty years, according to the funeral registers, and was buried on 4 January 1720 in the Nieuwe Kerk, at which point she disappears from history altogether.

Their bankruptcy must have been disastrous for the Fontijn and the Ten Grootenhuys families, but for this small, domestic history it rendered up an invaluable surprise: the archives of the Desolate Boedelskamer for 1692 turn out to contain a complete and extremely detailed inventory of the house on the Burgwal. After all the vagueness of previous years there is suddenly a description of the house that creates such an accurate picture it is almost as if on a June day in the seventeenth century someone walked through all the rooms with a video camera.

So let us join asset valuers Jan Pieterszoon Somer and Catharina Schoock on 27 June 1692, as they climb the steps and enter the house where, for a moment, life is frozen. First there comes a 'front house', with Spanish chairs, a carpet, and two large landscape paintings on the walls. Then we arrive at a passage with a wall clock and no fewer than nine paintings hanging beside it. On the hallstand we take note of two black worsted coats and an old hat.

Next to the passage is the inner room, with an alcove and an ornate bed valued at two hundred guilders, 'with purple damask hangings and white damask curtains and counterpane'. There is also a walnut cabinet full of the most valuable woollen cloth and damask. The walls are again hung with paintings: a landscape, two princes, a monk's face, an image 'being Samson's strength', plus 'two small pictures'. We walk back into the passage, where we come upon another cabinet, this one containing among other things 134 serviettes, 24 hand towels, 46 pillowcases, 56 maid's napkins and 16 neckties.

We move on into a room lined with gilded leather wall hangings. It too features an alcove with a bedstead – this time with a simple straw mattress – and there are six portraits on the walls, as well as a couch and another bed. The curtains are red, and lying on the wooden table are a Bible, a few colourful hats, some underwear and 'eighteen pocket handkerchiefs', as if the person who lived here suddenly stood up and walked away.

From the gilded-leather room we walk into the gallery, open on one side, which contains four simple chairs plus a table and two mirrors. Suddenly, writing this in the late twentieth century, it becomes clear to me where we are: in what is now my downstairs neighbours' kitchen dining room, where during renovation work we did indeed find a bricked-up passageway that must have led to the 'shed' in the garden.

We continue in the company of valuer Jan Pieterszoon Somer, whose mumblings were preserved for posterity by his clerk: 'a gown and a camisole, a lace jabot and three old hats, a variety of other rubbish, one guilder.' We come to a room with, according to the description, chintz wallpaper, two small mirrors, five portrait drawings, a board game (probably backgammon), a chafing dish for tea, a teapot and fifteen storage tins. We enter the pantry where are found tubs, copper kettles, boxes of candles, a plate rack and a copper warming pan.

Next is the stable. Many of the household effects described up to now will have belonged to earlier residents, but here we gain some idea of how the family squandered its money in those final few years. The place is stuffed full with the status symbols of the time: a coach, two carriages, a horse-drawn sleigh, something called a Mennonite cart, a hand-drawn sledge and two horses. Nearby must have been the servants' room: two beds, a few woollen blankets and five chairs. In the courtyard at the back of the house are two ladders, two buckets with copper fittings, twelve flowerpots, two small statues, a painted birdcage, a hand towel hanging up and 'a tin soap dish'.

The kitchen, as one would expect in such a rich house, is capacious: copper casserole dishes, pots, fish kettles, jugs, tongs, spoons, chafing dishes, and at the centre a simple wooden table (one guilder) with six simple chairs (one guilder ten cents). Beyond is a second pantry, whose stock includes a vat of wine and other supplies. The room nearby was no doubt the maids' quarters: two beds; green curtains. Higher up in the house is a back room where Jan Pieterszoon Somer finds a few chairs and a bedstead, plus a violin and a viola da gamba. The next room was the office. It must have been fairly large, as befits a trading firm of such stature: a big oak desk for the boss, a bench for the clients, five office chairs for the clerks, strongboxes, a harpsichord, a copper balance, and on the walls three maps, six landscape paintings, two still lifes, 'a painting being a Mary', another 'being nudes' and 'a work by Rembrandt' valued at twelve guilders (the other paintings were worth twice as much, on average).

Above all this were the lofts. In the peat loft was a huge supply of peat worth thirty-six guilders, as well as a gilded rack with several firearms. In the clothing loft some dirty linen was lying around: a couple of men's shirts, handkerchiefs, aprons and 'three neck-cloths' of the kind that were worn at night but also informally during the day. In the garret was a cradle, and in the rear garret an old cot.

We then move on to the part of the house inhabited by the elderly bachelor Jan ten Grootenhuys, and the contrast with the luxury of the De La Fontaines is striking. In the hall hang 'a black robe and a camisole', and in the cupboard are 'seven pairs of sleeve ruffs, with lace', a couple of undershirts and two nightcaps. That's about all. In Jan's bedroom are countless books, at least a hundred, and more are lying on the walnut table. They include picture books and a list of clergymen, and Jan Pieterszoon Somer notes that on a side table there are another 'nine books and papers'.

But Jan ten Grootenhuys' greatest treasure is something referred to as his book room, with two globes and a library of almost six hundred volumes.

The contrast between the couple and the bachelor is made even plainer by the inventory of all the books, which turns up in the same dossier after I move on a few pages. The library belonging to the De La Fontaine couple consists mainly of descriptions of the city, accounts of journeys to China, Rome and America, and titles along the lines of *Loyalty Must be Proven*, *Lives and Deeds of the Maritime Heroes*, *Cheerful Scenes of Today's World*, *Life and Actions of C. Tromp* or *Vondel's Tragedies*. Jan ten Grootenhuys' book room, by contrast, turns out to have contained a small but magnificent Renaissance library: letters of Erasmus, the *Imitation of Christ* by Thomas à Kempis, works by Jacob Cats, Brederode and Tacitus, *De Jure Belli ac Pacis* by Grotius and dozens of other juridical works, books with sea charts, and incunabula, including the commentaries by Venetian doctor of civil law Baldus de Ubaldis from 1492.

One thing becomes obvious immediately. Practically all the books date from before 1650. Of the entire list, only a handful of manuscripts were bought later. Even the library in which the down-and-out Jan ten Grootenhuys dozed in the declining years of the seventeenth century was probably not put together by him. The books and intellectual legacy of his grandfather, the high sheriff, spurred him on and inspired him. They were not his own.

3

Mathilde went to the piano and scratched to a powder a drop of wax that had dripped from the candles and congealed on one of the black keys. 'Yes,' said her father, who had gone to sit at the ta-

ble to read the paper for another half an hour. 'You really did play that sonata excellently, infinitely better than last time.'

'Ach,' she said, and immediately blew out the candles. 'Sleep well, papa.' [...] Upstairs she went over to sit on the window sill. It was a quiet, clear night. Short, playful gusts of wind blew gently through the trembling leaves of the trees that stood close to Mathilde on the embankment. The cobblestones under the streetlights wobbled soft-grey [...] Mathilde could see the upper windows and roofs opposite, sticking up above the trees. In one window, light was still shining, a steady dull light behind dirty yellow curtains. But Mathilde's gaze climbed higher, over the bluish and pale-red rooftops, up above the triangular and oval gables, looking far-wide, as if searching, into the gold-pricked luminous sky. The dark-green water of the narrow canal stole waveless softly past.

That is how Lodewijk van Deyssel, in his novel *Een Liefde* (A Love), describes the life of a father and daughter in a rich town house that – to judge by the few topographical details he provides – must have stood on the Oudezijds Achterburgwal. The atmosphere in our house on the Burgwal will have been roughly the same. From the archives we know that throughout the nineteenth century the house was occupied by people just like Mathilde and her father: the wealthy bourgeoisie, respectable industrialists, merchants and civil servants – typical representatives of the extensive middle class that over the years had come to set the tone in the city. For two generations the textile family Bonnike-Busch lived in the building. Then, in 1862, it was bought by an excise inspector, Johan van Someren Brand. From 1866 onwards a merchant and broker lived here, Conrad Pirsch. And in 1879 the house came into the possession of lodging keeper Ferdinand Jacobus Wierdels.

Anyone looking out over the city from one of its upper windows in the mid-nineteenth century would have seen what Mathilde saw: peace, silence and darkness. If we were suddenly transported back by some kind of magic to that sleeping Amsterdam, it would probably be the complete darkness that struck us first, the absolute blackness in which the city was wrapped when evening fell. Mathilde saw all the stars in the sky twinkling over the city. Streetlights were few, and when the moon was full they were not lit. The sounds were those of cartwheels and footfalls. Next we would be struck by the stench. A description of the city in those years speaks of 'revolting rubbish piles, dung heaps and suchlike' and of the unimaginably filthy canals, which at low water 'revealed their indescribable contents'. The city was regularly afflicted by cholera epidemics – in 1866 alone the disease claimed eleven hundred lives. One in every twelve Amsterdammers lived in a basement apartment. Child mortality was that of a developing country today. The average 'needy' worker did not live beyond thirty. On the corner of the Leidsestraat stood the remains of several houses that had collapsed in the early years of the century. No mansions had been built anywhere in the city for decades. The Golden Amsterdam of the seventeenth century had descended by the middle of the nineteenth into shabbiness and lethargy.

Its decline was slow and gradual. The active deal-making of the Coornherts and of Pelgrom van Dronckelaer became passive. Their children and grandchildren took things easy and lived off the interest due on their immense family capital. The money was invested in commercial enterprises, in land reclamation such as the impoldering of the Beemster and Purmer lakes, and in peat-cutting or the draining of peat bogs for cultivation in the provinces of Friesland and Drenthe. Foreign companies liked to come to peaceful, rich Amsterdam to borrow money, but in the second half of the eighteenth century the city increasingly lost out to London, trade was blocked by the Anglo-Dutch Wars, the harbours silted up, prosperity waned, and the final blow came when Amsterdam fell directly within the French sphere of influence in 1795 and remained within it for twenty years. That put an end to its position as a neutral trading city for good.

Yet tens of thousands of invisible threads still ran out from the weary eighteenth-century city to all parts of Europe, especially Germany. The family set-up that developed in the house on the Burgwal reflected the international relationships that were common among people of the higher classes. It began in 1738, when twenty-six-year-old banker Johann Breitenfeldt from Berlin moved in. He did not have a great deal of money, so he rented the house. Within three years other members of his family arrived and he also used the marriage bond to reinforce the commercial basis of his firm. By entering into a double marriage contract in 1741, he was binding himself firmly and irrevocably to his business partner and friend Frederick Gerard Loos. On 11 August he celebrated his marriage of convenience to Anna Agnes Visser, Loos' half-sister, in the house on the Burgwal, while on the same day, in Frankfurt, Loos married Breitenfeldt's sister Eva Maria.

Johann, Frederick, Eva and Anna lived in the house together from then on, in a kind of communal house-share, long before the term existed, and from a tax return of 1742 that has come down to us we can see that Anna's mother, widow Visser, moved in as well. Between them they kept two servants and had an annual income of 2,500 guilders. Loos died six years after the wedding, so in 1753 Breitenfeldt's young nephew Johann Ludwig Gregory came to Amsterdam to assist him and to train as a banker. Ten years later his uncle made the new recruit a partner in the firm – which was known from then on as Breitenfeldt and Gregory – and in 1766 young Johann married one Johanna Tack, who would bear him many daughters.

In those years of living off interest, when less and less was invested in the city itself and jobs were increasingly scarce, the gulf between rich and poor steadily increased. In 1778, in the magazine *Die Borger*, one enlightened writer sighed that society consisted of little more than people of independent means and beggars. Large segments of the city's population were impoverished and cast adrift; great gangs of them roamed the countryside. In the harsh winter of January 1763, for example, in a room in the Hoogstraat just around the corner from the house on the Burgwal, a woman was found with her three children, all four of them frozen to death. The mother was lying on straw in a closet-bed with two of the children, while the third child sat frozen stiff 'in a shitting chair'. Apart from the chair and the straw, there was nothing at all left in the room.

Meanwhile the Breitenfeldts and the Gregorys were managing to earn a good income as bankers of the enormous amounts of capital that remained in the city and needed to be invested. Breitenfeldt owned a stables and coach house on the Oudezijds Voorburgwal, a spirit distillery in Nieuwer Amstel called De Hoop and a house out along the river called Zeldenrust, which included a pleasure garden. But the house on the Burgwal was the centre of his little empire, a typical family home where parents, children, grandparents, grandchildren, uncles and nephews lived under the same roof for generations, eating from the same kitchen and at the same table.

Johanna Tack was an extraordinarily fertile woman. Within seven months of her marriage to Johann Gregory she bore him a son, who was named Jan Frederick after his late uncle. That was probably one of the reasons why they finally bought the house in 1768 – Breitenfeldt had rented it all those years – and rebuilt it in grand style. From records of the city's property taxes, and of course the accounts for the house itself, we can see the work that was done that year: an entire new storey was added and a new modern facade built, with neat rectangular windows and a straight cornice, new wide front steps, a carved stone door surround and an impressive front door. The passage was moved to the centre of the house and a new wooden staircase constructed, while the old stairs were transferred to the top floor to serve the attic. Up under the rafters was a big new loft, with warehousing space and hoisting hooks for the firm's commodities.

The hoisting mechanism is still there, as is the sixteenth-century staircase from the old house, once trodden by the Coornherts and the Van Dronckelaers. Hardly a trace remains of those eighteenth-century residents, however. We know that the Breitenfeldts died childless, and that the uncle left everything to his nephew Gregory and his large family. From 1789 onwards, Johann Ludwig Gregory, who had taken to using the Dutch forenames Jan Lodewijk, was a commercial privy councillor (*Geheimer Commerzienrath*) representing Prussia in Amsterdam, and in 1802 he was promoted to consul general. A number of letters have survived from the correspondence between Jan Lodewijk Gregory and the '*Durchlauchtigster Grossmächtigster*' king of Prussia, and they reveal that Gregory regularly supplied his monarch with casks of green herring and with kippers from Harderwijk packed in straw.

To judge by its style, the summer house in the back garden must have been built by the Gregorys as well. It is easy to imagine them drinking tea there in those years: mother Johanna in her wide skirts, the children, Gregory – he will undoubtedly have worn a wig – and perhaps old uncle Breitenfeldt too, since he lived until 1782. In one file in the archives I found a remarkable document that gives us a glimpse of their family life, and between the lines you can still hear suppressed giggles and larking about. It is a poem read out to Gregory by the children, onstage, in 16 October 1798 at the house of their uncle, Adolf Tack. It was on the occasion of the marriage of their sister Juliana to Jan de Burlett, by which time the family had moved to the Herengracht. Here are the final lines, spoken by the god Cupid:

Come friends! look straight ahead: the game is about to begin!
There lies the Bride undressed: the Bridegroom lies next to her
See! he lifts himself already a little at her side,
Look, look! how sweet, how soft, how tenderly they love!
Oh Sweetest Bride! you must presently go to it!
Praying won't help you here! no words can hold it back!
But no – you seem to fit yourself to the way the task goes.
Another moment now, mind you, and it will go differently.
(After the curtains around the bed have been closed completely)
Now look for the arrow that has struck both your hearts
And when you find it shout: 'Love is triumphant now!'
(A short pause, after which one hears in a tiny, refined voice from the back of the stage:)
'Love is triumphant now!'

In his epilogue, however, Cupid has something rather different to say. He confers on the young couple a blessing in which he talks about a 'happier time, when we are free of the fate that oppresses us now'.

It was 1798. The more relaxed style of the Patriot Movement had not passed the Gregory children by, but the arrival of the French Revolution in his own city in the form of the Batavian Republic must have horrified their father, the representative of Prussia. Eight years later, Holland was incorporated into France and the city gave up its proud town hall to serve as a palace for the new king, Louis Napoleon. Gregory's only good fortune was that he did not live to see that day. Johann Ludwig Gregory died in 1803, his wife Johanna in 1812, and where they lie, nobody knows.

Mere shards and fragments tell of the years that followed: a deed of transfer dated 1792; two rooms with an Empire ceiling. In the city's address book we find the name Lucas Anthony Bonnike as resident of the house, with a note that he traded in linen. He lived here with his daughter, who married a certain Busch and would move through the rooms and passageways for more than seventy years until her childhood home became the place of her death. Next there came an inspector of excises; then a merchant; a vertical extension to the back part of the house; a new zinc roof on the attic at the back; the lodging keeper; half-vanished frescos in the stairwell; and a strange kind of mural showing angels surrounding a primitive camera.

Lodewijk van Dreyssel's young Mathilde was a child of the old Amsterdam, that barely-lit city on which she looked out in 1860 or thereabouts, dreaming at her own window. But in retrospect that period was the start of a change in fortunes.

In the dark, silent, dilapidated city, something had begun to stir again, even if at first it was barely noticeable. The harbour's historical hinterland, Germany, began to modernize and it pulled Amsterdam along with it as it grew into an industrial nation. On the other side of the world, the Dutch East Indies were exploited with increasing skill and those colonial profits made it possible to finance large-scale public works back home: the laying of a network of railway lines and the digging of the North Sea Canal in 1883.

That latter project in particular marked the start of a second youth for Amsterdam; there was more work, labourers began to arrive in the city again and towards the end of the century that small trickle became a veritable flood of immigrants. According to the 1859 census the city at last had more residents than in the Golden Age, 243,000, and by 1900 the number had more than doubled to 510,000.

Amsterdam became a city of newcomers again, and the dynamism of outsiders and their thousands of invisible threads came back into play. Within two decades more major projects were undertaken than in the previous two centuries: the Central Station was built, then the Rijksmuseum, the Concertgebouw, the huge Paleis voor Volksvlijt, the Amstel Hotel; there were trams, telephones and the beginning of electrification; the harbour was extended with the addition of the long Handelskade; the Vondelpark was planted and new newspapers started up; there were trades unions and new political parties, and literature set off on unexplored paths.

The city broke out of its two-hundred-year-old walls, suddenly, in the space of a few years. All those new residents needed somewhere to live, and quickly. First to be built on were the former embankments and ramparts – those long apartment blocks in the Marnixstraat, for instance. Then the leafy Plantage was filled with housing and after that the first of the meadows around the city were raised with layers of sand: the Dapperbuurt, the Oosterparkbuurt, and even before that the area between the River Amstel and the Rijksmuseum, which became known as De Pijp or the YY neighbourhood, full of cheap rooms for newcomers, girls of easy virtue, artists and students – the Montmartre of nineteenth-century Amsterdam.

That was not all. The new Central Station closed off the centre of town from the IJ. The railways began to take over from barge transport, and within half a century Amsterdam was transformed from a typical riverside town into a land-based city. Several canals were filled in to give road traffic more space, but towards the end of the century the assertive nature of Amsterdammers came to the fore again: such a torrent of protest against this violation of their city arose that no town councillor has risked burning his fingers since. In 1899 there were briefly plans to fill in the canal in front of the house on the Burgwal, but almost all the residents on the waterside signed a petition to 'prevent the mutilation of the oldest and most distinctive part of town'. The signatories argued that 'should you wish to fill in every canal where people, horses or carriages have at some time met with an accident, not one would be spared in all Amsterdam'. In their opinion, 'recklessness among street youths and carelessness on the part of those involved are usually the cause of such unfortunate incidents'.

I am holding one of the earliest postcards of the canal, sent around the turn of the twentieth century by 'Ant.' and addressed to 'Mr L. Blauw, on the narrow road, Oud-Nunspeet'. The trees have been coloured green, the houses yellowish-brown and red and the canal grey-blue. The street is still empty and broad. It is just possible to make out the high double steps up to the front door of the house, next to the lamps of Hotel Stad Eberfeldt – particularly popular among travelling salesmen from the Rhineland and Westphalia. On the waterfront are several carts and a couple of boys observing the scene; outside the front door is a baker's barrow and next to it a man in a cape and top hat.

In the city's address registers, the main resident of the house from 1896 to 1923 is named as Adolph Goldberg, born in 1846. At first he lives there with one other man and two women; later they are joined by the Michaëlis family: two persons.

Goldberg is registered as the owner of a company that sold women's hats – the antique hatboxes we found during our rebuilding work must originate with him. He rented the house at first, buying it only in 1921. We also know that his already elderly sister-in-law Franziska Michaëlis lived there with them; those folders containing mournful pictures of pine forests that we found must have been hers. I suspect it was she who had the storeroom behind the house converted into a chapel, with a pulpit and an arched ceiling, with a dozen painted coats of arms, left and right, and with toilets for ladies and gentlemen outside.

There was something strange about the house in those years. The writer and historian Ben Sijes once told me that when he was a boy, at some point in the early 1920s, he was invited there for a meeting of a highly secretive society. He had to report to a hotel using a designated code word and he was led to the back, then leftwards into a passageway and suddenly he was in a room full of men and women. He didn't remember much about it. It was something like a Masonic or Rosicrucian gathering. The room was at the rear of another house, looking out onto a garden – he remembered that much.

During renovation work on the chapel we did indeed find an old passageway to the neighbouring house, permanently bricked up at some point in the intervening fifty years.

On 28 July 1928, Adolf Goldberg died and six months later his wife followed. The proceeds from the house now fell to his sister-in-law Franziska. His business was taken over by one Andreas Grasveld, who moved into the house with his wife Alida. Franziska died in May 1942 and Grasveld bought the house for the strikingly low price of eighteen thousand guilders. There was just one complication: Goldberg, Franziska Michaëlis and all their heirs and successors were Jewish.

Alida Grasveld died almost forty years later in the house on the Burgwal. On 10 October 1978 she was found by her family doctor, lying dead next to her bath. In her final years – she had been widowed more than a decade earlier – she lived downstairs, closing off the stairwell with a sheet of asbestos and abandoning the three upper floors to the mice, and to the snow and rainwater that came in through the leaking roof. She had difficulty walking, so she asked someone to screw handles onto some of the furniture, which enabled her to haul herself around her ancient dwelling with the strength she had left.

After her, a different kind of large family moved in, the kind that came into fashion here and there in the second half of the twentieth century: friends and acquaintances who had agreed on a communal house-share. They would create their own history with their own chosen family, a story of affection, rifts, friendship and indifference.

My image of the happy pre-war house was handed down by Annetje Wijnberg-Harvey, an English painter in her late seventies who had visited her uncle and aunt Dré (Andreas) and Aal (Alida) Grasveld regularly as a child. She still remembered the garden in the early 1930s, filled with roses, the hat company's large showroom on the ground floor, and the sitting room and big kitchen dining room above it, with dark furniture including a standard lamp and a heavy table where her aunt and friends always sat talking. The front facade was hosed down every Friday. The obscure room where those secret meetings were still held in her day was known as the Slaraffia. No one knew why. Her uncle was spruce, meticulous, always in a neat suit with a bow tie, her aunt warm and cheerful, rather stout, dressed in the latest fashions. Blackbirds foraged among the rose bushes.

After that everything changed. At the start of the Second World War, almost eighty thousand Jews lived in the city. By 1945 fewer than fourteen thousand were left. Almost a tenth of the population of Amsterdam was taken away never to return. The city had tried to protect them but in the end it let too many go: Amsterdam civil servants provided addresses; Amsterdam police officers did their duty; Amsterdam tram drivers drove trams packed with Jews to the Weesperstraat at night.

At the City Archives a bald, squarely-built man is leaning against a filing cabinet, reading some folio volume or other. He rocks back and forth, mumbling as he absorbs the text. He is blocking the way, so I ask him to step aside, but he only grunts, rocking, barricading the drawers with his body. Cautiously I touch him. His concentration instantly broken, he starts swearing in a muted library voice. His muscles tense and for a moment I think he's about to fly at me in the midst of the folios.

There is one remaining issue that I need to investigate: 1942. Jews. Eighteen thousand guilders.

At the NIOD Institute for War, Holocaust and Genocide Studies, the house on the Burgwal is among the buildings in the card index identified as being in the hands of an organization set up after 1945 to deal with property belonging to deported Jews. So something must have happened. There is also the information that one of the heirs, a Mrs Goldberg from Berlin, died in the camps on 23 December 1942. That is all.

From the deed of sale of 1942 it turns out that Andreas Grasveld bought the property not from Goldberg's heirs but from the Niederländische Grundstücksverwaltung, a Nazi organization that confiscated and sold Jewish real estate in the occupied Netherlands.

In light of all this, eighteen thousand guilders – the building was valued at more than that in the Golden Age – looks more like a sum intended to cover administrative costs than the actual sale price. Another file offers a few details concerning the estate agent who brokered the deal, Petrus van Bruggen. As early as 1933 he joined the Nationaal-Socialistische Beweging, the Dutch National Socialist Movement. He was active in a number of related organizations and made selling

Jewish property his specialty before fleeing to Germany when panic broke out among the Nazis and their Dutch collaborators on 5 September 1944 (a day known ever since as Dolle Dinsdag or 'Mad Tuesday'). His file in the archives of Bijzondere Rechtspleging (the court that was set up immediately after the war to sentence those guilty of high treason, treason or other war crimes) is at least fifteen centimetres thick.

I search through the file and slowly the picture shifts until precisely the opposite conclusion emerges. From an entry in the land registry it turns out that eighteen thousand guilders was not particularly cheap, given the neglected state of the building; the mortgage bank actually valued it at no more than twelve. A number of statements were included, testifying that Goldberg and his heirs always wanted young Grasveld and his wife to take over the business and the house. Their transaction in 1942 was the only way to keep it out of the hands of third parties.

Four years after the war, the sale was approved, retrospectively, by the official body charged with assessing all profitable deals made in wartime and returning property to its rightful owners where appropriate. For the Grasvelds that decision must have represented a kind of rehabilitation. But it will not have dispelled the mixed feelings that Dré Grasveld must surely have had about the shady National Socialist estate agent, and about the declaration of Aryan origin he was forced to submit while his own Aal was in hiding in the attics of the house because she too belonged to the chosen people.

He must have looked back on it all with resentment, sadness, and a strange kind of shame, the very feelings that have tormented and goaded the city ever since the time when its promise was broken.

God on the Prinsengracht

'As a child,' said the man from beyond Zaltbommel, 'as a child I once sat in a crate of mown grass, right down inside. I'll never forget it. The smell, the warmth. To me that was happiness.'

A great deal of ordinariness is required to make the extraordinary possible. And to enable a city to breath you need countryside. A lot of countryside.

At the average Amsterdam market – on the Lindengracht for example – many of the traders come from outside the city. The egg man is from Ermelo, the florist from Vijfhuizen, the poulterer from Putten, the fishmonger from Volendam, the baker from Zaandam. The greengrocers come down early each morning from Wormer and Beemster, and the cheesemongers drive up from somewhere near Woerden. Those places are the city's hinterland, the wetlands of its economy, and their activities diverge markedly.

Around 1540 the municipal worthies of Edam wrote that 'the city of Amsterdam is our capital city, of which we are the limbs'. The major conurbations and the surrounding countryside lived in something approaching a state of war for centuries and only in recent decades has that begun to change. Almost all the larger companies have moved to the outer suburbs, and the inner city has acquired a new function as the focus of entertainment and consultancy, a platform for cultural and commercial encounters and gatherings, the place for bankers and lawyers, accountants, advisers and advertisers, and increasingly the headquarters of companies whose operations are elsewhere. The great strength of the Western European urban centres is now their variety and their individual dynamism, and that certainly goes for a city like Amsterdam.

With rural areas further away the relationship is rather different. In today's Netherlands the system of subsidies and social housing is so extensive that we have little idea any longer of the real relationship between the city and, for example, the dairy farms of Friesland, the orchards of the Betuwe, the hothouses of the Westland or the pigsties of Brabant. But it is beyond dispute that villages producing only cheese, apples or beef cutlets for the city are entirely at the mercy of the whims and fads of city folk, to say nothing of technological developments. Who could have imagined forty years ago that French cheeses, Italian tomatoes and Spanish apples would be on sale in the Lindengracht market for the same price as products from Friesland, the Westland and the Betuwe?

Many rural economies are prospering, but at the same time they are brittle as glass because they were built on just one kind of product and stand or fall by its export to the city.

'It is as if the net of complete economic ties with which a city binds its own hinterland unravels at the borders of a city region,' writes the American expert on cities, Jane Jacobs. 'The various strands – markets, jobs, technology, transplants and capital – separate from the mesh and take off by themselves, each in its own idiosyncratic directions. In this fashion, cities shape stunted and bizarre economies in distant regions.'

As a result, the relationship between city and countryside has always been one of caprice and anxiety.

The places that supply Amsterdam are called Ureterp, Lemmer, Groningen, Tholen and Goeree-Overflakkee, but they also include Rhodes, Istanbul, Fes, Tétouan and Oujda.

The demand for travel and amusement on the part of contemporary city-dwellers has created extensive monocultures around the Mediterranean Sea that are becoming highly sensitive to fluctuations in the average Amsterdammer's holiday budget. Just as in the sixteenth century the city attracted workers from Waterland to do its heavy labour, and in the nineteenth century from poverty-stricken parts of Germany, like the city of Oldenburg and the state of Westphalia, so in the 1950s Amsterdam drew in thousands of workers from rural parts of Dutch provinces such as Groningen, Drenthe, Friesland, Zeeland and Limburg. In the 1960s and 1970s they were followed in their turn by men imported from Turkey and Morocco and later still by illegal immigrants from Eastern Europe and Africa. Without immigrants the great ships that sailed to the Dutch East Indies would not have been built or crewed, nor the nineteenth-century docks constructed, the roads repaired, the streets swept or the assembly lines manned. Although part of the city, they still carry the countryside within them. They feel the pull of the city and yet, within the safe walls of their own small communities, they keep the home fires burning.

Far from the city, beyond the high gothic tower of Zaltbommel and further out still, lives Paul. He resides with a friend, wife and child on a slight rise with three houses and an old mill, a hundred metres outside the dyke.

In winter, when the rain pelts down from a grey sky and the river is swollen, it's as if they live on an island. Everything around them – trees, fences, sheds – is under water and when it gets really bad you sometimes have to wear waders to get into the living room. But in summer the place is a little paradise, with chickens, sheep and goats, flourishing gardens, a small orchard, ships passing in the distance and a large table outside where you can drink home-made cider all day.

At the end of each week there's a whirl of activity in this small community. Hundreds of bottles are labelled and put into crates, and in harvest season boxes of freshly picked apples and pears arrive from all over the surrounding area. On Saturdays at daybreak, a small, heavily laden pick-up sets off along the dyke, first eastwards then northwards. The truck passes sheep, cows standing with their front legs half in the still water of an old arm of the river, cow parsley and buttercups, an old brick factory where eleven cats lie snoozing near the doorway, an ancient oak on a corner, and a white dyke house with a faded red musical stave on the front wall giving the notes of a forgotten song.

Paul has a stand at the Noordermarkt in Amsterdam. In the shadow of the Noorderkerk he sells his own 'Paradise Juice' made from apples and pears, his home-made cider, and often large batches of apples and pears as well. Occasionally he has plums, although that causes trouble, because the Noordermarkt is the most controlled market in the country: you can trade only in products you have made or grown yourself.

This farmer's market is a direct successor to the markets once found all over the city, every day of the week, selling milk, eggs, fish and vegetables, all of it brought in along the water-filled ditches that stretch far and wide, in hundreds of small flatboats crewed by fishmongers, greengrocers and dairymen. A nursery in Ommen sells plants, a grower from Ruinerwold brings fresh herbs, the cheese and eggs come straight from Wijnjewoude in Friesland, the vegetables from the Beemster and the Veluwe and next to Paul stands Jeanne selling wildflowers. One day I watched a Surinamese woman weighing a live chicken by the simplest method there is. She grabbed the bird by its wings and lifted it up, swinging her arm back and forth as she arrived at her estimate, and I suddenly realized: this is an act that hasn't been performed in this city for at least a century.

The market is a free trade zone between city and countryside, but only a few people earn good money from it. With her flowers Jeanne has a turnover of around two to three hundred guilders a week; when the costs are deducted that comes down to hourly earnings of around five guilders. On a summer Saturday Paul can earn about five hundred guilders, but he's hard at it for much of the week, and in winter the take is half that at best. Still, he always wanted to be a farmer, and Jeanne has never been able to do without flowers, all her life. Behind them a goatherd sells his small cheeses, from the sandy soils of Friesland. He has a herd of sixty white goats at home. In summer they graze in the open; in winter he keeps them in a deep litter house on a thick bed of straw. Milking twice a day, feeding, cheese-making, packaging, mending fences, mowing and spreading manure... The city people crowd around his stall tasting samples of his herb cheese, his charcoal ash cheese and his goat camembert. They go well with a dram, people tell each other, and they're delicious accompanied by a strong dessert wine.

A man comes up to Jeanne's stall and sticks his nose in between the bunches of wildflowers, sniffing as deeply as he can. 'Just like the old days,' is all he says.

At their backs, like a solid, protective wall is the Noorderkerk itself. It's old, unpainted and weather-beaten, but from behind the cracked walls you can still hear organ music every Saturday and Sunday. A young parishioner is outside on a ladder, attaching a banner to the rusted wall-ties above the door. An elder looks on. The banner reads, 'The church is open.'

The Noorderkerk is the last church in the city that still belongs to the Gereformeerde Bond, a conservative grouping that split from the mainstream Dutch Reformed churches in 1906. It's Tholen, Goeree-Overflakkee, Spakenburg and Putten in the heart of Amsterdam. On the street debates rage about free heroin or euthanasia, while within these walls people discuss the introduction of a little singing during services. Outside you can buy pornography at any tobacconist's, but inside this church all cohabitation by unmarried men and women is condemned out of hand.

Many members of the congregation were born and brought up outside the city, but not by any means all. 'If you don't need to work here, then as an orthodox Christian you get out,' some of them told me later, when I walked in now and then from the market. But others were rather more positive. 'Whatever else you may say, this lot around here do think about things,' said one of the girls handing out coffee.

The Noorderkerk was once a busy working-class church, but now, after the split with the Dutch Reformed, the depopulation of the inner city and increasing secularization, little is left of any of that. On paper they still have card-indexes full of members, but if as many as fifty are active I'd be surprised. Religion is as much a taboo in the city today as sex in the Victorian era. Yet everywhere there are groups, sects, niches and haunts where people still profess their faith, and in the Noorderkerk too, the congregation is growing again. One of the young churchgoers I came across even talked about it in military terms, using words like 'battle' and 'duty'. 'We stand here like Gideon's men in the front lines. This is the battlefront,' he said. We were in the doorway of the church on a Saturday afternoon in September, looking out over the market stalls at the men and women with shopping bags, the chatting couples, the shops, the cafés and the sheer, high house fronts on the Prinsengracht. The sparrows twittered in the afternoon sun, the trees were already yellowing slightly, but the market was still green: Michaelmas daisies, marguerites, colourful containers packed full of violets.

It was on a Sunday in November, at a quarter to ten in the morning, that I first attended one of the services. The weather was cold and grey, and the city centre existed only for seagulls, pigeons and the occasional lone Moroccan. Around the church it was deathly quiet and from outside all you could hear was the organ. The windows gave off a soft yellow light.

At that moment a darkly dressed woman hurried across the square, bent over the pram she was pushing. A second child was sitting below the handle. They were singing something, and as they came closer the child began humming more loudly and the mother sang along with him, to the notes from the organ, running, emitting fragments of a psalm, panting behind the jerking pram, 'Come go with us, do as we do.'

We slid in through the door at about the same time, through the old porch, into the church. The pews are arranged around the pulpit as if at an army camp, high and enclosed on the outer edge. Once you're inside them they form a cosy ring around the pastor.

The rest of the Noorderkerk is a huge empty space, with grey pillars, redbrick walls and an undulating floor beneath which hundreds of forgotten Amsterdammers are buried. In the corners, behind partitions and railings, lie the remnants of other churches, covered in dust: seats, benches, even a pulpit from a vanished house of God, lying on its side.

In one specific sense the Noorderkerk is unique: it is one of the few listed buildings in the city that has not been restored. Anyone wanting to know what a church used to look like in past centuries will learn nothing from the shiny, polished Westerkerk, or from the Nieuwe Kerk, which has been converted into an upmarket party venue. Only in the Noorderkerk do the doors still creak. The bellows room behind the organ is just as it was when it took three burly men to pump enough wind into the instrument, and even the cabin hooks on the toilet doors date from the nineteenth century.

In its glory days the church must have been a beautiful building and in certain places you can still get some idea of what it was like. This was one of the first churches in Europe to be designed specifically for Protestant services, with a central pulpit, a huge oak roof and excellent acoustics. In the nineteenth century it was tampered with quite a bit: the pulpit was replaced, the exquisite old chandeliers were sold and the beautiful oak vaulting was coated with thick layers of grey paint. Yet the church still has something of the private, intimate atmosphere that leaps out at you from the paintings of Johannes Vermeer and Pieter de Hoogh.

In essence the Noorderkerk has always remained a product of the seventeenth century – and I don't mean the building alone. The sermons are of oak, the Bible is read in the 1637 translation, and as to the newfangled thinking of Huub Oosterhuis, not an iota of that has ever penetrated the church.

Today's pastor can make the dusky vaulting resound as it did three centuries ago, and he uses it to the full. 'Magnificent,' he whispers into the microphone. 'Magnificent,' he says out loud. 'Magnificent!!' he roars into the booming church and the congregation sits rigid in its pews. He doesn't fight shy of politics – Russia, South Africa, he works through them all. 'When you walk across Dam Square or sit in the tram, don't you find yourselves thinking, "Sheep without a shepherd"?' he whispers. Then, raising his voice: 'Three per cent of Amsterdam still goes to church. Ninety-seven per cent has no church any longer. No one cares for their souls. You can counsel them, but no one can help them through the Narrow Door.'

Outside everything is still murky grey. Christmas is in sight. The church is freezing cold. Beneath the yellow light of the chandeliers sits the congregation, silent, two hundred and fifty souls, the men black or grey in their coats, the women wearing hats, a few students, here and there a deaconess. A girl at the front stifles a yawn. The pastor talks about 'sin' and 'idol-worship with Ba'al'.

'We pray to You for the city in which we live,' he says. I do something I'm not supposed to do, I look around during the prayers. The elders are sitting with their eyes firmly shut. Some people have put one hand over their face. A few have their heads deeply bowed, almost touching the pew in front.

Only the children are looking. Almost all the children are looking. They peer around, smile and wink at each other. It's as if a dusty toy cupboard has come to life in the church, and for a moment there's one grand conspiracy of surreptitious peeking. After an hour and a half they are all outside again, happy and shivering in their coats, the same church, the same people, the same faces as when Johan Braakensiek sketched them on a winter's day around 1890 outside this door. Except that now we are living a century later, and everything has changed.

There is no greater cultural divide in the Netherlands, or indeed in Western Europe, than between town and countryside. Yet countless Amsterdammers need only to go back one or two generations in their family history to come upon a time of transition from the land to the city: parents who left the province of Twente shortly after the war because Amsterdam offered them more opportunities; a mother who moved here from Drenthe as a child because her father's farm had gone bankrupt; grandparents who decided to escape the poverty of the hedgerow landscape of eastern Friesland at the end of the nineteenth century. One by one they were torn loose from their families, customs and traditions – ruptures of which the consequences can sometimes be seen to this day.

If anything has determined the character of this city over the centuries, then it is the phenomenon of immigration. In the late sixteenth century, Amsterdam filled up with refugees from the Southern Netherlands, most of them Jews and people from Antwerp on the run from hunger and the Spaniards. Then later came the Huguenots and later again German traders. In the period 1880 to 1900, seventy-five thousand people left the three northern provinces of the Netherlands, most of them heading for Amsterdam, and from then on there was a continual influx from all parts of the country.

It was an internal migration that continued, with peaks and troughs, into the 1950s. Then the exodus of families ended. Agriculture had emptied itself of people and the difference in wealth between the western region and the rest of the country was no longer so stark. Most importantly, the Dutch began to have other priorities besides work and income, such as living in a nice place where you felt at home. Still, single people kept coming, as they do to this day. Anyone in a village in Groningen who divorces his wife is likely to take that step, building a new life in Amsterdam and the same goes for a girl in the Achterhoek who quarrels with her parents, or a young man in Brabant who discovers he is gay. Of the many Amsterdammers in their early twenties, three quarters were born and bred elsewhere. There is hardly a resident of the city who doesn't carry the heart of an immigrant within him.

Everyone has a different story of transition from rural to urban life. In the 1920s an analysis was published of hundreds of letters from Poles who emigrated to America. The authors, William I. Thomas and Florian W. Znaniecki, were sociologists, and the changes they observed are largely the same as those seen by anyone who moves from the countryside to a city, whether he comes from Friesland or Morocco. We read in those letters how, for example, immigrants slowly began to see their own, individual existence as more important than the fate of the family. Ideas about money and pleasure changed too. It was no longer regarded as immoral to spend money on pure enjoyment – something that is fairly normal in a city but conflicts in all kinds of ways with the caution and frugality of life on the land. The letters also show that the pursuit of success, a strong current in every large city, became increasingly important, in sharp contrast to the acceptance of the status quo that emerges from the letters written back home on the farm. Lastly, the researchers found evidence in the correspondence that norms and values gradually changed from 'qualitative' to 'quantitative'. In other words, immigrants and their children began to find the nature of an object less important than, for example, its price.

So those Polish letters could have been written by any immigrant to a new city. Every one of them struggles for years, sometimes for generations, to adjust his or her traditional norms so that they somehow fit with the dynamism of urban life. Sometimes a kind of compromise is found. Sometimes there is a flight into drugs or drink. Sometimes an immigrant becomes totally isolated, or creates a private world from which, if only for a few hours per day or per week, the city can be shut out.

After the service in the Noorderkerk, a great diversity of people will always stand talking and drinking coffee on the broken, undulating gravestones: ordinary members of the congregation, some from Amsterdam, many from elsewhere, along with, for example, an Armenian family, a former drug addict and a Greek Orthodox woman – at least so it was on the Sundays I joined them. One old lady confided to me that she was actually a Lutheran, but she liked coming. 'They're good to you here when you're elderly. There's love here.' She'd been a regular churchgoer at her old church, but it had closed. 'It's a mosque now, I believe.'

Organist De Vries came down and started to tell me all

about the organ. He was an organist above all else, he said, just like his father. 'You didn't go to hear the sermon, you went to play the organ.' But from behind the green curtains he'd heard everything. What things were like before the Gereformeerde Bond was formed. The old church where the smell of peat poured out to greet you in winter. The empty church: 'One time we had a service here and including the pastor and the elders there were fourteen people.' The sixties church: 'We once heard a tape recording of an unmarried mother. Very sad, yes.' The choirs: 'They didn't add anything and just made everyone late.'

I got chatting with an elder called Bruggeman. 'Look,' he said. 'If we did things here the way they do on the Veluwe we'd have no chance at all in this city. Of course you have people here who still think women shouldn't wear trousers, but you'll find extreme types wherever you go.'

His wife, from Utrecht, said, 'At home we weren't allowed to cycle on Sundays. Yes, that's the kind of family I come from. It was all laid down, "you must do this and you must do that." ' She found life in Amsterdam a breath of fresh air. 'Living here you realize that God is far more merciful than you ever imagined. He's not an ogre. At home a lot of things were major issues that are side issues for us. We try to keep the commandments, it's not live-as-you-like, but it's more of your own free will.'

Still, I asked, what about unmarried mothers? In the past they wouldn't have had it easy in a Gereformeerde Bond church. 'Don't be silly,' said Mrs Bruggeman. 'I would say, "Come here, child!" ' And what if a young man discovers he's homosexual? Mr Bruggeman replied, 'I'm not in favour, no. I can't approve, my Bible teaches me that. We try to be of help.'

Mrs Bruggeman told me about her daughter, who has a homosexual friend, an unbeliever, too. 'He's been a visitor in our house for years. A fine young man.'

What about living together before marriage? Mrs Bruggeman's response was immediate, 'Wrong, wrong. As it happens, a boy from the congregation rang me only yesterday. His girlfriend was visiting from Groningen. He asked whether she could stay with us. He didn't even want to give the wrong impression.' 'If people are living together we try to end it,' Mr Bruggeman added. 'In fact we once put up a young man for months. He married here.'

We discussed bars, cinemas and other worldly matters. Even in the Noorderkerk those things stopped being taboo years ago. 'You form your own opinion, and at a certain point you'll stop of your own accord,' the Bruggemans said. Their daughter came to stand with us. 'My circle of friends is 100 per cent secular. They don't understand it at all, but they certainly don't object. A Sunday like this is a wonderful day of peace. See, they expect you to be one of those dull types in a long black dress silently working away in an office, but I look normal, and I do normal things, and they think that's weird.'

In his youth elder Bruggeman went through one period that he didn't really want to talk about. It was just after he left home, in Amsterdam. He didn't go to church for a while. 'I came from a very closed environment, you know.' He paused. 'I went out and explored the world a bit, as it were,' he said eventually. 'It was very different then from now.' He seemed a little embarrassed, 'I sometimes went out for a drink after work with the others.' Another pause. 'I went to the cinema a few times too, and to the theatre...'

Some lengths of carpet had been laid on the stone floor

against the worst of the cold. We were all wearing thick coats and warming our hands on our plastic coffee cups. The children ran around the pulpit. Suddenly a real drama threatened. The pastor's youngest son couldn't find a Matchbox car that he'd been given by Sinta Klaas a few days before. Consternation all round. But it was quickly found again, jammed between two gravestones on which the names had worn away.

One morning I went to visit the pastor of the Noorderkerk at his home in a quiet backstreet in South. His congregation came from all over, he told me, everywhere from Uitdam to Watergraafsmeer. While other churches were emptying, they, the strictly orthodox, were experiencing growth, although he had to admit that a great many young people no longer attended church, 'They bow before the storm. There are hardly any intact families left here, almost everyone laments the loss of a son or daughter.'

They were trying to hold on to the young people and nurture future leaders through confirmation classes, youth groups and a coffee bar. One major problem was finding suitable marriage partners. Most of the young people did eventually marry within the church, but it was difficult to meet a Christian girl. One way to do so was to attend the Windroos conferences, organized by the mainstream Reformed Church youth group, the Hervormd-Gereformeerde Jeugdbond.

His congregation usually read the daily newspaper *Trouw*, with its Christian ethos – 'they find it too left-wing' – and the *Reformatorisch Dagblad* – 'too right-wing'. Most had televisions, usually to watch EO, the evangelical network, although a few preferred NCRV, another Christian broadcaster. The life they lived in the city could hardly be described as isolated either; they included teachers and nurses, students, several police officers and a man who worked on the ferry that crosses the IJ.

'As people we have to learn to belong to a minority, with minority beliefs and minority morals,' he said. 'From time to time I'll receive a phone call from the Veluwe or Zeeland, "Pastor, our son needs to move to Amsterdam to study. Do you perhaps know of a room where he'll be safe?" Sometimes a boy like that is in the gutter within a week.'

His congregation was much better armed against that sort of thing, he felt. 'They're orthodox, but they're Amsterdam orthodox.'

I notice the distinction when I find myself at the church's weekly coffee bar one Friday evening. Some twenty young people are sitting in groups of five, ploughing through Judges 7. 'Whosoever is fearful and afraid, let him return and depart early from Mount Gilead.' I introduce myself to a few of them, and then I'm allowed to join in.

Gracia, a girl of fourteen, sighs and blows a bubble with her gum. 'Here lies the beginning of prophesy,' says Chris seriously. Gracia puts her face in her hands. Richard prays, 'Lord, we thank you that we may meet together every Sunday in your house.' Gracia leaps to her feet, because now it's time for the game.

The game goes like this: the girls sit on chairs, the boys stand behind them, one chair is empty and the boy there, winking, has to try to lure a girl away from the others. This results in endless running around, clutching, screeching and whinnying. 'Grab the shoulders only!' Richard calls out.

It's followed by table tennis and shuffleboard. Next week

they're all going to go bowling and have a meal together, and once a month an evangelist comes with a guitar and they sing. They've put on a record with a real swing to it. 'Gospel music,' says Chris. 'We only have gospel music here.'

At the bar, meanwhile, a vehement discussion has erupted about psalms and singing. 'Hymns don't come from the Bible, so we're not allowed to sing them during church services,' Chris explains to me. 'What nonsense,' the young man next to him exclaims indignantly. 'That means we must never sing about Jesus, because all the psalms are from before his time.' 'If they don't want something in the church, they always say it's in conflict with the Bible. "Slippery slope", that's the favourite term here, and "out of hand".' 'The conservatives can block anything. Everyone's afraid of starting a row.'

Gracia is standing in a corner with three other girls, all of them rocking and swaying. They're mimicking Candy Dulfer.

'And the waves pound against the hulk of the church. And the faithful listen and tremble. Because they so need the sustenance of the faith.' The evangelist is reading from a tract. I've stepped into a community centre called Hebron in the Spaarndammerbuurt and the open lunch for isolated people in the neighbourhood has just finished. Forty men and women are sitting at two long tables. Most are elderly, but there are a few children running around. They sing, 'What a friend we have in Jesus.'

On the tables are bread, fruit, apple syrup, processed meat and chocolate flakes. The room looks like a church in miniature. Some of the women are wearing slippers, their thin elderly legs encased in brown stockings. Many of them are knitting. A woman with a stick walks back and forth. Others are busily sweeping and scrubbing the floor.

In a corner sits a young man with an aquiline nose and a full black beard. He's studying a Bible text with the utmost concentration. He reads, 'If there is then any comfort in Christ.' He whispers, almost singing softly to himself to accompany the words, his upper body rocking involuntarily forward and back.

We're going to sing from the old Hymnal for Households and Gatherings published by the trading company Johannes de Heer and Sons in Rotterdam.

Swishing past the clouds is
A lovely name

and:

Above us there is a delightful place
Oh so beautiful, Oh so beautiful!

A woman with bandaged, swollen legs is helping to serve coffee. A slightly confused lady calls out continually above the hum of voices, 'Coffee guzzlers! Coffee guzzlers!' The evangelist delivers a short sermon and then it's time for questions. 'Things sometimes go a lot better for unbelievers than for believers. Why is that?'

The dachshund belonging to one of the women breaks free. 'What did God do with people before Jesus was born?' The evangelist says he doesn't know anything about that. 'But they were definitely very godless, weren't they,' a man says. 'That flood wasn't for nothing.' 'There have been films about it.'

Next to me sits Mr van Boven. We get talking. All his life

he was employed by the council sanitation department, but now he's been declared unfit for work and he's spent the past few months in a psychiatric hospital. 'I had such a panic, you know, on Saturday. My heater exploded. Fire brigade came. Fire. Fire everywhere.'

He asks if I'll write a statement for him, saying that he's had words with the woman next door, and that he admits it, but that he couldn't help it, he was in such a panic. The fire brigade witnessed it all. Yours sincerely, P. van Boven.

It's Sunday again. I have permission to accompany organist De Vries. He walks up the narrow steps to the organ. He was early, as usual, and in his car he killed time by listening to the police radio. He mutters as he looks at the thermometer next to the organ. Five degrees. He pulls open a series of stops: the bourdon, the prestant, the stopped flute, the vox humana and quite a few others. Leaning forwards in his thick winter coat he starts to play. 'When it's really freezing I sit on each of my hands in turn and play with the other.'

The congregation sings: 'God be merciful unto us, and bless us, and cause his face to shine upon us.'

While we sit at the organ waiting for the reading, De Vries tells me he loves the old-fashioned, non-metrical psalms. 'Sometimes I slip in an extra one. Beautiful.'

'We have subjected ourselves to being humbled by you,' says the pastor. Below us sits Gracia, angel-blond. She yawns. De Vries adjusts the stops, looks through the curtains briefly and taps the thermometer. 'Up by one degree.'

A member of the congregation edges towards Bruggeman. 'Hey, go and take a look, would you? There's such a blast of cold air coming out of the heating grid it's ridiculous.' Bruggeman creeps into the cellar in his dark elder's suit and pulls a few levers. Five degrees again.

'Oh Lord into your hands we...'

'Commend our spirit,' says De Vries. 'I'll just get some wind into it, we'll have to start up again in a moment.'

'And now a few announcements from the church council. On Saturday 19 December we'll be singing carols on the Noordermarkt. Do all try to join us. The floral greeting goes to...'

'Come on, get on with it,' De Vries mumbles, and during the final few sentences he holds his arms above the keys like two huge wings before sweeping them down as soon as the pastor has finished speaking.

The building is silent again. Hands are together or in front of the eyes. The pastor prays, 'Over the past week we have wandered astray like lost sheep. Even though we have sinned, Lord, come and find us. Confused though we may be, like a sheep in the undergrowth...'

Outside there is no one, apart from a cat distrustfully crossing the street. Clouds pass overhead, grey after grey. On the roof of a houseboat stands a dishevelled heron, motionless. The trees are bare, the window boxes arid, and in the doorways lie the last of the dead leaves, brown and wet. High up on a hoisting hook is a pigeon, as if waiting for something, head pulled in, its feathers fluffed up against the wind.

The forgotten girl, the city and the painter

The young girl was hanging from the post like a lifeless doll, crossbeams to her left and right, a strap under her armpits, ropes around her baize skirts, her right hand raised slightly by the gibbet and next to her, dangling, an axe. The IJ lapped at her feet and her face was turned towards the city. When the elderly painter saw her for the first time, she had already been dead for some hours. On that day in early May she was strangled in front of the town hall on the Dam before her body was carried over the IJ to the Volewijk, where the ferry now moors, to rot slowly in the sun and rain.

The painter drew everything precisely. With great attention to detail he recorded the cut of her clothes, the ropes around the slight bulge of her belly, her feet hanging in midair, the hem of her skirt as it moved in the wind, her minutely lop-sided mouth and those closed eyes that give a rather childlike cast to her face. When he'd finished he went to stand over to the right of her and started drawing her again, in profile this time. He drew nothing of the surroundings, neither the landscape nor other corpses, he drew only her, in close-up – unusually for him – as if he wanted to preserve something of her innocence for eternity.

Those two drawings by Rembrandt Harmenszoon van Rijn now hang in the Metropolitan Museum of Art in New York, and thanks to detective work carried out by Amsterdam archive specialist Isabella van Eeghen we now know the identity of the young girl. Art historians had always believed the 'girl on gibbet' was from an earlier period, but it was actually a relatively simple matter to find out precisely when she was drawn, since the work, after all, depicts a historical event. 'Elsje Christiaens of Sprouwen in Jutland, 18 years old; says she had been in this city for no more than 14 days,' is how case number 84 begins, heard before the city magistrates on 28 April 1664 and noted in one of the Confession Books, many of which have been preserved in the city's archives.

It is fairly easy to work out from the handwritten account just what went on during Elsje Christiaens' brief stay in Amsterdam. She arrived in mid-April, intending to find work as a maid. For the time being she moved in with a landlady on the Damrak, hoping to be able to pay for her lodgings when she received her first wages. After two weeks, however, the woman suddenly asked for a thaler (2.5 guilders) for the bed, a sum the girl did not have. The next morning at half past seven, the landlady again started demanding a thaler and threatened to confiscate the few belongings Elsje had brought with her. Elsje refused to pay, the landlady began hitting her with a broomstick and Elsje, 'in her fervour', grabbed an axe that was lying on a chair and attacked the landlady with it. The blow knocked the woman down the cellar steps and she lay there dead. Then Elsje smashed another lodger's trunk open with a hammer, took some linen out of it, put that down again and removed a worsted coat from another trunk. She told the neighbours, who had stormed into the building in response to all the shouting and screaming, that the blood on her hands was from a nosebleed. She managed to get away. The neighbours, on finding the dead woman in the cellar, set off after her. In a panic Elsje jumped into the water of the Damrak, but she was immediately caught and soon afterwards she appeared before the magistrates.

The records I have before me now date from her court appearance, 'She says she became extremely anxious because the woman was no longer willing to keep her. She says that the woman's husband left 14 days ago.' Many so-called landladies of this kind were in fact brothel keepers, which may help to explain the furious row between Elsje and her victim. I can find no reference to prostitution in the entry in the Confession Book however, even though there was another cross-examination the following day – she confesses everything once more – and on May 1st, a further note, 'She admits to having taken a coat and linen from trunks belonging to others, but knows nothing about any money or a cap brooch' (it seems other items had been stolen as well). The verdict is written in the margin. 'To be strangled at a post until dead, and to be hit on the head several times by the executioner with the same axe that she used to kill the woman.'

It is not clear on what date Elsje Christiaens died. Perhaps it was that same first of May. It will have been no more than a day or two later. Rembrandt must have taken a boat across to the gallows field almost immediately after the execution, as in his drawing the girl's corpse is still fresh.

When Rembrandt had himself rowed across the IJ to draw Elsje Christiaens' body, he was no longer the successful painter who used to hold court with his apprentices on the Jodenbreestraat, in what is now the Rembrandt House Museum. He had grown old, the second great love of his life,

Hendrickje Stoffels, had died not long before, and a few years prior to her death he had moved to a small house on the Rozengracht, number 184. He now lived in the large district that had been developing since the early seventeenth century on the western side of the city, as did most of his fellow painters. Carel du Jardin lived not far away, Govert Flinck had a splendid house on the Lauriergracht with an impressive exhibition hall for his work and Pieter de Hoogh, Gabriël Metsu and the poet Joost van den Vondel lived just around the corner. They had all followed in the wake of their rich clients to live in the new residential districts on the city's outskirts.

Within a single generation the look of Amsterdam had changed utterly. The population had risen from fifty thousand in 1600 to around a hundred and fifty thousand in 1650. Tens of thousands of immigrants from Antwerp, Portuguese Jews, later the Huguenots from France and migrant workers from Germany, along with the original inhabitants – they made up a metropolis that must have had the same power of attraction in those days as New York has in our own.

A large painting of the Dam in 1652 by Johannes Lingebach shows the Amsterdam public of the time: merchants from all points of the compass, three of whom are even wearing oriental robes, ship's captains, dockworkers, drummers, pedlar women, notables, beggars, and behind them the long row of houses on the Warmoesstraat and the tower of the Oude Kerk. From the *ondertrouwregisters*, the lists of those who registered an intention to marry in the city, which represent a good cross-section of the population, it seems that for a considerable period more than half of Amsterdam's young brides and bridegrooms came from out of town, as many as 73 per cent in 1611 and 1615. The great majority of immigrants, more than fifty thousand of them, came from Poland and Germany: peasants from Schleswig-Holstein and Ostfriesland hoping to find work as labourers or sailors; craftsmen from Bremen; and Jewish traders from Poland uprooted by the violence of the Thirty Years War. In the seventeenth century, out of a city population of 200,000, no fewer than 51,591 Amsterdammers were immigrants from Germany, East Prussia or Silesia.

It gave Amsterdam the dynamism of a city of outsiders, of people who had shaken off the Middle Ages and were profoundly attached to their new city yet still maintained relations with countless cities, towns and villages across Europe through a web of written correspondence, trading contacts, friendships and family ties. It was a place of the here and now. 'In this city there is no man who is not involved in trade,' said French philosopher René Descartes in about 1635. 'Everyone is so intent on his profits that I could spend my whole life without being seen by anyone.' There were few churches, palaces or other imposing old buildings, and what struck practically all visitors was that everything in the city was geared towards financial gain. The Amsterdam of the 'golden' seventeenth century was one great money-making machine. Every suitable location, every hand capable of work of some kind, was used for the purposes of profit.

It is still possible to catch a glimpse of the townscape of those years when arriving by train, in between the buildings along the banks of the IJ. The first impression made by seventeenth-century Amsterdam on anyone arriving by sea was that of a forest of masts, pennants and towers. There were windmills on the quayside and cranes pointing into the sky, and in the foreground the water teemed with rowing boats and sailing craft. Beyond them, formal and stately, were the quarters where the sea captains lodged, on the Zandhoek and the Buitenkant, the present-day Prins Hendrikkade. On the many jetties, dockworkers and merchants were everywhere, and at the water's edge you could buy milk, eggs, straw, quicklime and whatever else had been rowed over from the countryside of North Holland on the far side of the IJ. The smaller ships sailed up the Damrak, in front of Elsje Christiaens' boarding house, where they unloaded their wares. The great seventeenth-century merchant vessels were too big to enter the city, so they anchored in deep water alongside the palisade in the IJ – where an island was built for the new Central Station in the late nineteenth century – and had their goods brought ashore by lighters. The largest ships of all, the East Indiamen, sailed to Amsterdam only for major repairs. They usually docked out on the shipping lanes, at the island of Texel off the country's north coast, where their loads were transferred to and from smaller vessels.

Along the gentle bend in the IJ, three kilometres in length, a complete water landscape had been created, divided into paths and fields by landing stages, with large ships tied to posts and countless smaller ships bobbing about on the fields in between. This waterscape had a structure all its own and there were even a few wooden buildings supported on piles, as if they had wandered astray among the ships: shipping company offices, a platform with two strange-looking wooden cranes, guardhouses, dredges, the 'gate bell', which was rung each evening when the booms that closed the city off from the waterside at night were about to be lowered and a special 'city inn', a large wooden building, to accommodate non-residents who had arrived too late to be allowed into the city. The atmosphere of this strange, lapping, half-rotten world is recreated again and again in old prints and drawings: crooked mossy posts, gates, jetties and steps, the silent water, a rowing boat, a scattering of seagulls. For centuries this place marked the transition from city to water – until the construction of the Central Station finally closed the city off from the IJ for good.

Elsje's boarding house stood at one of the busiest spots in the Amsterdam of her day. It was, and remains, the point of arrival for most travellers, so it was natural for her to take a room there. Ships' captains congregated in and around a building at the head of the Nieuwe Brug, where they paid their harbour dues and took on new passengers and freight. In an adjacent office, sheets of paper were posted up with the arrival and departure times of all the ships in the harbour. The city was served by an ingenious transport system, with barges and tugs that came and went, punctual to the minute, day and night, covering the whole of the Dutch Republic. There were daily services to roughly twenty-four destinations in the provinces of Holland and Friesland, some even departing several times a day for towns like Haarlem, Enkhuizen, Workum, Alkmaar, Hoorn and Leiden. The hourly service between Amsterdam and Haarlem alone served some two hundred and fifty thousand passengers a year, many of whom were on their way to destinations further afield. So the departure points were always crowded with barrow-boys, businessmen, evangelists and touts for boarding houses and other facilities.

A German, Filips von Zesen, who visited Amsterdam in the same period as Elsje, wrote a travel account, and he was clearly astounded by the commotion, a deluge of sound that struck him on the Damrak. First he saw the corn exchange, built over the water in the form of a square, with a wooden colonnade all around it. There the merchants took handfuls of grain out of crates and assessed its quality against the northern light, carefully, taking their time, because their profit lay in the smallest of details. But everyone knew that the deals being done concerned tons of cereals, warehouses full of grain, ships and half-cities, sometimes even war and famine.

A little further on was the Dam, and you could hear the criers of the fish market there from a considerable distance away. The Damrak stretched to the place where the National Monument on Dam Square now stands, and there too, ships lined the quay. In front of them stood the Waag (the weigh house), headquarters of the civic guard, where people were always milling about because all goods traded wholesale had to be weighed there to assess the amount of city tax due on them. The building was demolished in 1808, after the king of the time, Louis Bonaparte, said it spoilt the view from his palace.

On the other side of the Dam was a second exchange, the commodity exchange, built over the water of the Rokin. It was a large stone building with covered walkways around an open courtyard where the merchants gathered, and an upper floor with shops where all kinds of luxury items and curiosities were sold. 'It seems as if almost the whole world gathers here to conduct business,' Von Zesen observed. It was frequented by Dutchmen, Germans, Poles, Hungarians, Frenchmen, Spaniards, Muscovites, Persians, Turks and even Indians. The noise was deafening and at every pillar wares of a particular type were traded: tobacco, silk, jewellery, bills of exchange, shares, real estate, comestibles, hides – some four hundred different articles altogether. Anyone could get anything, including entire art collections or loans for the building of palaces. Monarchs and princes could even purchase whole fleets of warships. The destinations posted up here covered the whole of the known world.

Since 1609 the city's exchange bank had been housed in a side wing of the town hall on the Dam. It was an invention of the municipal authorities that made Amsterdam's trade appreciably easier. Countless different coins were used in every trading city, so international trade could be awkward, even chaotic, when it came to payment. By means of the exchange bank the city took over the function of general bank teller. Unfamiliar money could be valued there and exchanged for sound, widely-used currency. A pouch of English guineas, a handful of French *louis d'ors*, a gold ingot from the West Indies – they could all be exchanged for a stable monetary unit made of paper: the *banco florijn*. A bill of exchange from this bank, actually an early form of banknote, would be accepted by every merchant in Amsterdam. The city guaranteed absolute discretion, as well as full access to the money deposited as soon as it was needed. The exchange bank was the lubricant to Amsterdam's trade and it was famous throughout Europe.

Around these centres of trade some ten different newspapers were sold, containing lists of prices and business bulletins that furnished information about where the fleets were, what kind of loads the trade caravans were carrying, and the condition of the harvest all over the world. As early as 1618 the world's first regularly published newspaper appeared in Amsterdam: the *Courante Uyt Italien, Duytschlant etc.* owned and edited by Gaspard van Huten. Later the *Tydinghen uit Ver-*

scheyde Quartieren (Tidings from Various Quarters) by Broer Janszoon would grow to become the first proper press agency, its economic reports eagerly received and distributed by merchants worldwide.

The strength of this great edifice of capital, trade and information lay above all in its speed and reliability. The merchants on the city council kept a close watch on the quality of services rendered. A captain arriving in Amsterdam knew immediately where to deliver his load; a trader could operate in the city with the strangest of coins without any trouble at all; a merchant could be certain that reports from abroad contained no deliberate distortions. Continuity, efficiency and trustworthiness – that was the key formula behind the economic miracle.

Standing high above it all on the far side of the Dam was the brand new town hall, later to become the royal palace. It was finally completed in 1662. In the years in which Amsterdam grew to become a world power, the modest mediaeval council chamber had remained the centre of all plans and activities, but on 7 July 1652 a devastating fire put an end to that old building for good. Gone were its tower, arches and big wooden statues of the counts of Holland.

The new building was designed by painter and architect Jacob van Campen (1595-1657), who was strongly influenced by the classical Italian style, and it was of a size unprecedented in those years. Everything about it spoke of the city's power and wealth. Rising high above the houses, rivalling the nearby Nieuwe Kerk, its exterior was sober and stern, but inside was an opulence never seen in the city before, beautifully ornamented arcades and courtyards, and a huge Citizens'

Hall as elegant as anything in Venice. There were dozens of offices, workspaces, and rooms for burgomasters and aldermen. The attics included a large arsenal for the civic guard and the cellars a cell complex for convicts. The entire seventeenth-century governmental enterprise was lumped together in a single stone colossus.

At the same time, its extravagance was placed firmly in a moral context. There were no statues or paintings without some hint of a wagging finger. Above the entrance to the Desolate Boedelskamer where bankruptcies were administered, a fresco can still be seen showing Icarus as he fell. Reliefs in the Aldermen's Hall feature biblical scenes, urging good and just government. The paintings, which include works commissioned from Rembrandt, tell of the sober and unimpeachable rulers of biblical times and classical antiquity. The burgomaster of Amsterdam could not walk into any of the rooms without being reminded that he was the descendant of a skipper or a stocking merchant, and that his fortune was neither more nor less than God's grace, which might just as easily turn against him.

It was at this town hall full of gilded sermons that Elsje Christiaens met her end. The death sentence was pronounced in the Hall of the Court of Justice, with its great bronze doors. Her execution took place, as did all capital punishments, on a wooden scaffold in front of the building – in the facade traces can still be seen of the square notches into which the beams were slotted. She spent her final hours in the cells below, which adjoined the dungeons and torture chambers.

'All contemporaries are as one in praising Amsterdam as the place for commerce, the temple of trade,' writes French historian Henri Méchoulan in his book about the mentality of the city in the seventeenth century, *Amsterdam au temps de Spinoza*. 'But first of all Amsterdam should be seen as the cradle of freedom.' Genoa, Venice and Antwerp were also important and wealthy mercantile cities, but, he writes, they never brought about a revolution in the European consciousness. The Amsterdam that emerged after the bloodless revolution of 1578 was a new city, created by a formula for success never previously tried, the pursuit of wealth combined with the new concept of liberty. Here, for the first time, money plus freedom drove out the old mediaeval pairing of honour and heroism, and with them the idea that the greatest virtue lay in conquest, in war, the knight, the king and the court. 'It is therefore a victory for those who profit daily from the market, where trading is the source of power, living a life that can flourish only when freedoms are put to use,' Méchoulan writes. 'The first of which is unquestionably the freedom to "persevere in being oneself".'

To an important degree the foundations of modern, humanist, enlightenment thinking were laid here, and to regard the famous Dutch tolerance as purely a product of the 1960s is to betray an ignorance of history. As early as the sixteenth century, Dirk Volckertszoon Coornhert took a stand against Calvinist extremism. In a long series of writings, he advocated freedom for all expressions of faith and for all schools of thought, and universal peace through moderation and tolerance. Along with Erasmus he is regarded as one of the founders of European humanism.

Frenchman René Descartes, 'the father of modern philosophy', who arrived in the city in 1629, was another of those who found here the peace and freedom he needed to gather a following. It was in the Netherlands that he developed his theories on rationalism, for instance. He believed that this mathematical form of reasoning could be applied to non-mathematical areas of life, and by doing so he laid the foundations for a way of thinking that shapes the Western world to this day. Half a century later, in that same Amsterdam, British philosopher John Locke wrote his *Letter Concerning Toleration*, building on ideas first set down by Descartes.

Finally, there was a boy who must have played right outside the door to Rembrandt and Saskia's house, who grew up to become one of the most important philosophers of all time. Baruch de Spinoza was born on the Houtgracht near the Breestraat in 1632, over behind Rembrandt's home. His father was a rich Portuguese-Jewish merchant, but because of his independence of mind and his heretical beliefs, Baruch was expelled from the Sephardic congregation while still a young man. A spiritual exile, he began a lifelong quest for the foundations of truth, freedom and moral wellbeing. He was an eternal outsider, which only made him all the more fervent a participant in the public debates that took place in this new city of immigrants and citizens. His views about whether or not a 'true' religion existed, and about the need for a tolerant state, free of interference from any church, remain pertinent to this day.

Whether the clever boy from that busy Spinoza family looked up to his neighbour Rembrandt we will never know, but there is a fair chance that he did. In seventeenth-century Amsterdam, painting was by far the most popular art form. The city had no courtly culture and no aristocracy, the Church had almost ceased to function as a patron of the arts, and artists therefore had to rely on the well-to-do citizenry. The wealthy of Amsterdam usually wanted a picture on the wall, nothing too expensive but nevertheless something that would elevate their status. 'Tronies' (intriguing faces), landscapes and biblical scenes were produced in a constant stream, often by anonymous painters for an anonymous market. Their work was no longer anything like as meticulous as it had been in previous centuries, and the freer artistic style sometimes made it possible for a painter to produce more than one work in a day. Paintings therefore became cheaper, and they were simply sold at the market along with chairs, tables and chickens. 'All in generall [strive] to adorne their houses, especially the outer or street roome, with costly peeces,' wrote Englishman Peter Mundy during a visit to Amsterdam in 1640, and he added that he had even seen paintings put up in shops by bakers and butchers, or indeed blacksmiths and cobblers.

The move across town by the Amsterdam painters' colony clearly indicates that the market was growing, and also that the elite was gradually relocating from the centre of town to the periphery. That process would continue in the centuries that followed until, after moving to the area around the Vondelpark and the district beyond known as South, the wealthy eventually took up residence in Buitenveldert, Amstelveen and Bloemendaal.

In 1600 most artists still lived in the heart of the city, close to the Dam, in the area around what was then called the Pijlsteeg and would later become Damstraat. Paintings had always been traded by town messengers or in the junk stores that were concentrated here, and it was in this same Pijlsteeg that many of the brothels were to be found, which supplied the painters with models. Of the boys growing up in the centre of town, quite a number became artists, including Pieter Lastman.

In the early seventeenth century the art trade moved to the broadest part of the Sint-Anthonisdijk, the later Breestraat, now the Jodenbreestraat, where there was still space for the Amsterdam regents and rich immigrants from Antwerp to build spacious new houses. The street soon became what Gary Schwartz describes as an industrial district for painting. Pieter Potter and his son Paulus Potter, both painters, moved into a house near the new Anthonispoort (beside what is now the Jonas Daniël Meijerplein); Pieter Lastman had his studio opposite the Zuiderkerk, where Rembrandt studied for six months in 1624; Cornelis van der Voort, who painted Laurens Reael, lived near the sluice on the corner of the Zwanenburgwal, close to the production studio of art dealer Hendrick Uylenburg, who, incidentally, barely knew how to hold a brush.

In 1631 Rembrandt took over de facto leadership of Uylenburg's painting factory, and he and his apprentices created and copied paintings non-stop. In the four years that he worked for Uylenburg, Rembrandt painted at least fifty portraits of prosperous citizens, and his popularity rose even further when he started using his Frisian wife Saskia – Uylenburg's niece – as a model. The charming Floras, shepherdesses and courtesans sold hand over fist. Meanwhile the painter's relationship with Uylenburg cooled, and a year after his marriage, in 1635, their collaboration ended.

The district had a profound influence on his work. Rembrandt biographer Gary Schwartz has calculated that all his most important patrons, clients and dealers, from Pieter Lastman to the reverend Joannus Uytenbogaert, from Hendrick Uylenburg to Jan Six and the Trip family, lived within the four hundred metres that separate Rembrandt's house from the Waag on the Nieuwmarkt and in the six hundred metres between the Waag and the Kloveniersdoelen.

In January 1639, Rembrandt bought a fine merchant's house next to Uylenburg's studio, the building that is now the Rembrandt House Museum. In 2002 a cesspit was excavated in the courtyard of the house and there the archaeologists found all kinds of items the great master must have held in his hands, including fragments of earthenware vessels, pots of dyes and pigments, and small tobacco pipes. For his pupils Rembrandt fitted out a warehouse on the Bloemgracht as a studio and painting factory, which meant that like most other painters he was again moving in the wake of the elite, this time to the Jordaan, the neighbourhood of the labouring classes and small tradesmen, where all activities were concentrated that were banned in the belt of canals. Eventually, in 1658, he would go to live there himself. The Jordaan, with its little narrow streets, was built at the same time as the spacious Herengracht and Keizersgracht, so the neighbourhood for dirty fingernails was born along with the neighbourhood for clean hands, although they did not spill over into each other as they once had. They were kept separate, with the Prinsengracht between them like a river, as was the intention from the start.

Segregation between the main belt of canals and the Jordaan typified the altered social relationships within the population of the city. Back in the time of Father Wouter Jacobszoon, Amsterdam merchants had generally stored their wares in their own attics. Their lives were played out amid shopkeepers and small tradesmen, and they worked at home or in their own backyards. Although some rich merchants lived in Amsterdam in the sixteenth century, the wealth of the average trader was not particularly great. The tax records for 1585 show that Dirck Janszoon Graaf, a dealer in iron who became burgomaster, was the richest resident, with a fortune worth 140,000 guilders (the equivalent of several million euro), and there were no more than five Amsterdammers worth 100,000 guilders. By 1631 their number had increased twentyfold.

Within a single generation, a new type of merchant emerged in Amsterdam, and most of the capital accrued to him. He was a trader who, at the commodities exchange and elsewhere, dealt in goods that he never laid eyes on, indeed his wares sometimes had yet to reach the city. He invested huge sums in enterprises of which he had no understanding at all. The draining of three large lakes in North Holland, for example, to create the Purmerpolder, the Schermerpolder and the Beemsterpolder, was typical of the projects financed by seventeenth-century investors, who also put up money for costly expeditions to unknown worlds such as the East Indies, America, Tierra del Fuego and the North Pole. The new type of merchant introduced a new kind of status, and a new form of intellectual development.

This quiet social revolution came about in the early years of the seventeenth century. In 1600 the average merchant still lived among ordinary citizens, but not for much longer. As historian Ed Taverne wrote long afterwards, in his study of the development of the city's main seventeenth-century canals, 'The merchant-patrician, later barely aware of the origins of his authority and power, became estranged from the people, withdrew from the overcrowded city centre and settled in an exclusive neighbourhood, the belt of canals that was laid out from 1615 onwards.'

So Amsterdam created for itself just that one urban monument. There were no grand squares, private estates or palaces but instead something quite different, the showpiece of a rich, independent and self-assured bourgeoisie: its own exclusive residential area.

The building of the city's famous belt of canals therefore marked the end of Amsterdam as a place where residence, work and other aspects of life were combined. Ever since, people in the different districts of the city have gone their separate ways. Rembrandt was an exception in that sense; he was an old-fashioned Amsterdammer with strong ties to his own neighbourhood. In the Breestraat he could pluck his biblical figures straight off the street – the Jewish district was right around the corner – and a contemporary described him as someone who was always strolling through the markets:

searching avidly on the Nieuwemarkt and Noordermarkt
for suits of armour, helmets, Japanese daggers, furs
and pleated collars that he deemed worthy of painting

They were all destined for his studio, where he often composed scenes in the way a stage manager might. In his famous 'The Prodigal Son in the Tavern', for example, Rembrandt plays the main role himself, dressed in finery with a rummer of wine in one hand, while his wife Saskia takes the part of a strumpet. He is radiant and in high spirits, she a little doubtful, looking round at us as she sits on his knee. Early Rembrandt experts saw merely a moralistic wagging finger, but perhaps the painter is holding a mirror up to himself. He kept this painting rather than selling it, which in itself fuels the notion that through play-acting and disguise, Rembrandt was actually playing himself all along, and goading his audience.

The painter and art historian Arnoldus Houbraken, who was taught by a number of Rembrandt's pupils, described half a century later how Rembrandt used paper and tarpaulin to close off separate little rooms for his pupils where they could 'draw from the life'. One hot summer's day, the model and one of the apprentice painters 'undressed stark-naked'. The other pupils were standing peering in at the scene through a tiny crack when Rembrandt arrived. First he too stood and watched, but when the pupil said to the model that they were now 'like Adam and Eve', he banged on the door with his maulstick shouting 'In that case, out of paradise now', and he chased the pair down the stairs, still half-naked.

As will have become clear by this point, Rembrandt was a true craftsman. At its peak his business was a fairly large studio enterprise and as a result, all kinds of studio scenes from Rembrandt's painting factory have survived: groups of pupils sitting around a model, drawing; a pupil with two models and the master who has come to take a look; and a delightful depiction of the atmosphere of Rembrandt's private studio in his house on the Breestraat, showing an easel in the foreground, light streaming in through a high window, a table by the window with a lectern that was used for making etchings and drawings, to the right a cradle with the blanket drawn back, and next to the fireplace a half-undressed woman, probably Hendrickje Stoffels.

Over the course of his working life, Rembrandt had more than fifty pupils or assistants, which is one reason why, in the past, quite a few paintings have been wrongly attributed to him. After he became fashionable, he systematically built on his success and cashed in. He is known to have visited auctions where, if need be, he drove up the price of his own works. There is a story that he once bought an etching of his 'Christ Preaching' for the then enormous sum of a hundred guilders at a public sale, purely to ensure that his works remained expensive and rare.

In that endeavour he had a fair degree of success. A portrait from his hand – such as his painting of Andries de Graeff, who later became burgomaster – cost five hundred guilders. In the case of 'The Night Watch' he was paid a hundred guilders for every figure depicted. It made him one of the highest earning painters in the city. His etchings, soon distributed across many European collections of prints, brought him international fame. So for most of his life he was not a lonely genius but a fashionable painter who set the tone in the Amsterdam canal belt year after year.

By the spring of 1664, when he drew Elsje Christiaens, all that was over. In the self-portraits of his later years we see a heavy-set man wearing a painter's cap, grey haired, with tired, rather puffy features. His sharp gaze has grown more distant, observatory rather than challenging. In his wanderings around Amsterdam – especially after Saskia's death – he sometimes made a few sketches and drawings, but the core of his activity was in his studio.

When he had himself rowed across to the Volewijk on that day in May, he was therefore departing from his routine in all kinds of ways. It was rare for him to leave his studio, and his drawing of Elsje looks different from all his other work.

With extraordinary precision, he did his utmost to record everything about her, as if attempting to freeze time, halting her death and decay for a moment. At the same time he gave both drawings an air of resignation and empathy, creating a memorial to Elsje's youth that would transcend the fate that had struck her down.

The body of Elsje Christiaens was immortalized again a few weeks later, by the painter Anthonie van Borssom. He painted the entire Volewijk gallows field, including all the corpses that were hanging or sitting there at that moment: two men on the great stone gallows (the court records indicate that one of them had been hanging there for three years), a corpse attached to a post with a spade next to it, the remains of a murderer on a wheel with a pistol above him and, at the far right, clearly recognizable, the post with the axe and the body of Elsje Christiaens. We can see the colours too now. Elsje is wearing a red baize skirt and a grey jacket. Her body has sagged down somewhat in the intervening weeks, so that her head is at least half a metre lower than in Rembrandt's drawing.

Elsje Christiaens was sentenced, as we read in the Confession Books, 'to be consumed by the air and the birds'. She was to be 'fixed to a post with an axe above her head', which is exactly what happened. From that same Confession Book we know which men interrogated Elsje and decided she should die. Their names are scrawled under the first interrogation, the alderman-magistrates Burg, Blaeu, Rochus van de Capelle, Van Loon, Spieghel and Bronckhorst. We can easily trace the ancestry of most of these gentlemen. Dirck Spieghel was from one of the oldest Amsterdam families, grandson of a herring buyer, son of a soap-boiler on the Nieuwendijk and himself a director of the West India Company and boss of the crossbow shooting gallery. Nicolaas van Loon was a merchant on the Keizersgracht and governor of the House of Correction. Vincent van Bronckhorst belonged to another rich merchant family. Coenraad Burg, former ambassador to the tsar of Russia, was a director of the West India Company like Spieghel, as well as being a senior administrator of the Amsterdam colony in New Netherland, North America. Blaeu was none other than the famous cartographer Joan Blaeu, responsible for the immensely valuable nine-volume *Grooten atlas ofte wereltbeschrijving*, better known as his *Atlas Maior*.

Each of the men who determined Elsje's fate was therefore a textbook example of the seventeenth-century Amsterdam patriciate. They were members of an elite that set the tone in the city in all fields of activity, a new family-based network that governed trade and shipping, as well as having a firm grip on the reins of the municipality. We are familiar with their satisfied faces from countless portraits, including the captain of 'The Night Watch' (future burgomaster Frans Banningh Cocq), Dr Nicolaes Tulp of 'The Anatomy Lesson', burgomaster Andries de Graeff, the Trip family, Jan Six, and the Bicker brothers.

Take for example Vincent van Bronckhorst. He was a highly respected merchant on the Keizersgracht, but the real money came from his father, one of the merchants who in 1595 had sent out captains Cornelis Houtman and Pieter Keyser with four ships to seek a new trade route to the East Indies, independently of the Spanish and Portuguese. The East Indies were an unexplored region. In 1592 an enterprising clergyman called Peter Plancius had got hold of twenty-five Portuguese maps showing 'all the sea coasts of the entire surface of the earth', with their depths, shallows, cliffs, harbours, as well as the secrets surrounding the routes to the East and West Indies, the characteristics of foreign peoples and the wares they had to sell. This information was invaluable to the Amsterdam merchants. Secretly, on Plancius' initiative, they sent an envoy to Lisbon – probably Cornelis Houtman himself – to garner further information about the route to the Indies.

On 2 April 1595 the little fleet sailed out of the IJ and more than two years later, on 14 August 1597, three of the four ships appeared again before the palisade near the Schreierstoren. Of the two hundred and forty-nine crew, only eighty-seven had survived the voyage, and the profits of the enterprise were less than impressive. Yet the returning sailors were greeted as heroes. They had found a viable route. The greatest commercial enterprise the city had ever seen could now commence.

Bronckhorst's father was a director of the New Company on the Sailing Route to the East Indies. Such companies were powerful institutions, the PLCs of their day, by means of which Amsterdam merchants financed all sorts of risky enterprises. Because the risk was spread, they ventured a great deal. In 1602 this particular company grew to become the world's first ever multinational, the Dutch East India Company. In the two centuries that followed, it would control all trade and shipping to Asia. Its head office was at East India House in the Oude Hoogstraat, now part of the University of Amsterdam, and contemporaries said you could smell the cloves and nutmeg from many streets away.

An organization like the Dutch East India Company was virtually a state within a state. Its all-powerful directors were able to trade, in the name of the Dutch Republic, with the powerful tribal leaders of the Indies, and even to build their own forts and recruit their own troops.

In 1621 a second company was established, again to combat the supremacy of the Spaniards and Portuguese but this time in the Atlantic Ocean. Called the West India Company, it established a small trading post on the River Hudson in 1624. 'The Lands were as pleasant with Grasse and Flowers and goodly Trees as any they had scene, and very sweet smells came from them,' runs one of the first reports about the island, named Manhattan. It was the start of the settlement of New Amsterdam, which later became New York City.

The WIC traded mainly in sugar, tobacco, pearls, furs, tropical timber and ivory. A great deal of money was also made from the transport of black slaves from West Africa to the plantations of America. Between 1626 and 1650 alone, some seventy thousand slaves were shipped out, one in five of whom did not survive the passage. From 1683 onwards, Suriname was exploited as a private colony by the city of Amsterdam and by the Van Aerssen van Sommelsdijck family. Along its great rivers, one sugar plantation after another arose. An estimated three hundred thousand slaves from Africa were taken there in the course of the seventeenth and eighteenth centuries, to perform the heavy labour. The entire project was directed from West India House on the Haarlemmerstraat. The building still stands and is now in use as a venue for parties and receptions.

There was a third company too, the Northern or Greenland Company, founded in 1614, which specialized in whaling. At first the merchants had tried to avoid the hardships of the usual route to the Indies via the Cape of Good Hope by searching for a new passage via the polar region, but three expeditions failed and no further attempts were made. One crew of an Amsterdam ship, captained by Willem Barentszoon, set off in 1596 and spent a harsh winter on the polar island of Nova Zembla. As a result, it became known that many whales swam in polar waters, which meant blubber and whale fat, soap and lamp oil, a fresh source of profits.

The motive for all this was not avarice alone. The maps by Joan Blaeu, with their strange geological formations, distant islands and approximately drawn coastlines no longer inspired fear but presented a challenge. Large blank patches demanded to be explored, in fact the entire world was begging to be discovered and studied, from the microcosm of a water droplet to the Terra Incognita that was North America. Joan Blaeu brought all that within reach, making it tangible, knowable and available for transformation. The companies were therefore in a sense a national adventure in which everyone could take part, although Amsterdam clearly had a central role. The names of more than a thousand shareholders are recorded in the registers. They include prominent merchants, but also craftsmen, clergymen, schoolmasters and servants. These huge commercial operations were an expression of the daring and dynamism of an urban population that sensed it was on the threshold of a new era.

It was that same dynamism that drew outsiders like a magnet. For Elsje Christiaens, hoping to enter service, Amsterdam was an obvious place to choose. While real wages were falling all across Europe, they were rising in Amsterdam. In Cologne a labourer earned some fifteen stivers a day, in Arnhem twenty-two and in Amsterdam twenty-seven. There was little to be seen in Amsterdam of the extreme poverty and hopelessness that afflicted the rest of the European proletariat in the same period. Because the city held a key position in the grain trade, bread prices were stable. A three-pound rye loaf cost around four and a half stivers, which meant that the ordinary man had enough money left from his daily wage to pay for a little luxury and variety: fresh vegetables, butter, cheese, eggs and fish. At the city's markets all those things were available in abundance, and they were relatively cheap.

Rembrandt, too, as a newcomer from Leiden, quickly found employment. Through Hendrick Uylenburg he gained access to the city's highest circles. He painted pastors, burgomasters and shipping magnates, became a member of the Saint Luke's Guild for painters and moved into his own splendid merchant's house on the Breestraat. His marriage to Saskia van Uylenburg provided him not just with many happy years but with additional status and income. He had an extensive collection of rocks, coins, Roman busts, helmets, drawings, prints and rarities to rival the collections of merchants and patricians. It is indicative of the relatively open society of seventeenth-century Amsterdam that craftsmen such as Rembrandt (a painter did not yet bear the stigma of the artist) could easily be accepted into higher circles. His 'Night Watch' – the painting was so named only much later, because the dark varnish became so dirty it looked like night-time – was immediately seen as a clever and daring piece of work because of the unusual arrangement of the militiamen.

Rembrandt was a man who went his own way, and a perfectionist to boot, but people were prepared to put up with that. Houbraken heard later from his pupils that their master would sometimes spend two days 'adorning a turban to his liking', whereas in other parts of the picture he could be extraordinarily slapdash, applying colours to the canvas 'as if with a coarse tar brush'. Sometimes the paint seemed 'as if it was smeared on with a bricklayer's trowel'. When visitors tried to look at his paintings from close proximity he would hold them back with the words: 'The smell of the paint might offend you.' 'As for his nude women,' Houbraken added, 'the most delightful subjects for the artist's brush, [...] they are too wretched to sing or to play about.'

Rembrandt never used a 'Greek Venus' as a model, complained another contemporary. It was always a washerwoman 'or a turf-stomper from a barn'. He took not the slightest notice of art critics. On display in New York is a satirical sketch by Rembrandt in which all kinds of fashionable gentlemen admire the latest work in an artist's studio. One of the visitors is wearing a hat with two enormous donkey's ears sprouting from it, and off to one side of the canvas sits the painter himself, laughing and defecating into a pot. Amsterdammers took it all in good part. Rembrandt's artistic freedom was regarded as a form of freedom of conscience. No one in Amsterdam opposed the right of a citizen to do and think whatever he liked in the privacy of his own home – as long as he did not overstep the mark in his social dealings.

I fear that Elsje Christiaens merely stood stammering and stuttering when faced by those powerful Amsterdam gentlemen. It is noted in the Confession Book that she came from Jutland, from a little town called 'Sprouwen'. Yet when I tried to reconstruct something of Elsje's life, if only by investigating the place she was from, the trail immediately ran cold. In all of Denmark there is no Sprouwen to be found.

A Danish-speaking friend suggested there might have been a small, sad misunderstanding. 'Sprog' and 'sprow' come from the same root as the Dutch verb 'spreken', to speak, and there is a good chance that Messrs Bronckhorst and company simply did not understand what she said. If she answered the question as to where she was from by saying something in Danish like 'But I don't speak your language,' then it might very well have been noted down as 'Sprouwen'. Elsje was therefore recorded as coming from a little town called Whadidyasay? Later a description reached me of a tiny island just off Funen called Sprogø, rendered in mediaeval handwriting as Sprowae. Notorious for being a robbers' den, it had been on lease to Dutchmen for years. But whichever it was, Sprogø or Whadidyasay, for Elsje the outcome was inevitable.

Rembrandt's relations with the city's elite were more complicated. Like Elsje he was a newcomer, a simple miller's son from Leiden who had attracted attention at a young age for his remarkable talent yet never quite made it to the top. Like most of the members of the civic guard depicted in his 'Night Watch' – rich cloth merchants who contributed to the city's prosperity and became deacons or orphanage governors but had no influence beyond that – Rembrandt would never penetrate the top echelons of Amsterdam society. In the almost forty years during which he was one of the most prominent portrait painters in the city, he painted only three members of the city council, for example, and never a sitting or former burgomaster. Rembrandt expert S.A.C. Dudok van Heel, in a study of the role played by this miller's son in Amsterdam social life, concludes that in his lifetime he was never referred to as "sir", the form of address for the patrician class. He remained a painter-dealer trading in art. Elsje Christiaens' immigration came to nothing, and in the end even Rembrandt remained an outsider.

Not that the city was closed off in that sense. There were plenty of immigrants who did make their way to the top, although often not for one or two generations. Take Vincent van Bronckhorst, one of Elsje's judges. His grandfather was a brewer in Weesp, his father a grain merchant on the Warmoesstraat in Amsterdam, and he himself belonged to the highest social stratum of all, with a fortune worth a hundred thousand guilders. After serving as a judge he became a justice in the Supreme Court of Holland.

In total, 174,874 immigrants arrived in Amsterdam from other countries in Europe in the period 1601-1800, and another 153,490 from the Dutch provinces. In 1600 the city had a population of about 50,000, in 1622 105,000, in 1630 120,000, in 1650 some 160,000 and from 1700 onwards the population wavered around 220,000. The marriage registers speak volumes. Between 1646 and 1650 only a third of brides and bridegrooms were born in the city. A quarter were from elsewhere in the Netherlands, mostly from the provinces of Gelderland, Brabant and Friesland, while more than forty per cent were from the Southern Netherlands, Scandinavia and, in very many cases, from Germany. In other words, the influx of migrants that had started in the late sixteenth century for religious reasons had by the mid-seventeenth century assumed the character of an international network of workers, craftsmen and specialists. All this must have given Amsterdam the feel of an American city, a place where you could rise very quickly but fall just as fast. That latter fate would strike Rembrandt as well.

Elsje Christiaens died to the continual ringing of the town hall bells, watched by crowds of ordinary people who had poured onto the Dam, but no eye-witness report of her death has come down to us. No doubt the gentlemen of the bench – Burg, Blaeu, Rochus van de Capelle, Van Loon, Spieghel and Bronckhorst – would have watched from a prominent position. The executioner received the standard tariff of six guilders and there were no burial costs because 'the earth was not granted her' as the expression went. As far as the city was concerned, the case had been settled.

As for Rembrandt, several decades after his death the great masterpiece now known as 'The Night Watch' was transferred, along with several other large paintings of companies of civic guards, to a new position in the Amsterdam town hall. It was allocated the smallest space, between two doors, and to make it fit it was trimmed on all four sides. Two guards on the left were removed and on the right a drummer was cut in two, so that only his head, arm and drum remained. The canvas then slowly grew dark with dirt and dust.

In contrast to the time-honoured image we have of him, Rembrandt's decline had little to do with poverty or lack of recognition. When Saskia died in 1642 he was rich and famous. Houbraken calculated that from his many pupils alone he was earning twenty-five hundred guilders per annum. For years he had enjoyed an excellent relationship with the young merchant, writer, patron and later burgomaster Jan Six. Rembrandt made etchings for him, and plates for the family album, sold him three of his paintings, borrowed money from him and painted his portrait. Six tried unsuccessfully to entice Rembrandt into the life of Amsterdam society, but in 1654 the friendship suddenly cooled. Six sold Rembrandt's debt to someone else and when he married in 1656 it was Govert Flinck who painted the bride's portrait. We can only guess at the reasons for the rift.

In retrospect, Rembrandt's fall off the societal ladder was probably caused by social faux pas more than anything else. That same insolence that made 'The Night Watch' so striking wrecked his relationships with Amsterdam's upper crust.

First of all there was Rembrandt's character. To put it mildly, Rembrandt was not a particularly nice man. Almost without exception, the few anecdotes we have about him illustrate his miserliness (his pupils painted coins on the floor as a joke, to make him bend down), his foul temper, his moodiness, his rudeness and spitefulness. Gary Schwartz points convincingly to the silent witnesses in all the documents we have about him: no one ever asked him to be godfather to a child, or to testify in a legal dispute, or even to supply an expert valuation of a painting.

Secondly, Rembrandt had no firm political base in the city. The Amsterdam socio-political network rested largely on a system of patronage and protection. The status of a painter was determined only in part by the quality of his work. More important was the question of which circles patronized him – just as today museums and art critics determine the 'value' of an artist. In that sense Rembrandt drew an unlucky hand. The most powerful group of Amsterdam patricians, the Bicker family, never ordered a single painting from him. When, for reasons that remain unclear, Rembrandt fell out of favour with the Court of Orange after Saskia's death, his prestige in the Amsterdam salons took a knock. Portrait commissions ceased to come his way. True, after 1650 a number of patricians came to power who had been among Rembrandt's clients in the past – Frans Banningh Cocq in 1650, Joan Huydecooper in 1651, Nicolaes Tulp in 1654 and Andries de Graeff in 1657 – but his most highly placed client in those years was a mere alderman, Joan Jacobszoon Hinlopen. He lost out on all fronts to the top Amsterdam painter of the time, his pupil Govert Flinck, an artist who had excellent connections with the Oranges, the Brandenburg court and the ruling patrician families, although little now remains of his fame other than a slightly shabby street in De Pijp.

There was more to it than that, however. From surviving documents it turns out that Rembrandt seriously violated the unwritten rules of the Calvinist patrician families in at least two instances: one a case involving domestic morals, the other an issue of business ethics.

The domestic matter concerned a sordid affair involving Rembrandt's housekeeper Geertje Dircx. She had been taken on to look after little Titus, but soon after Saskia's death the painter began a relationship with her. He would not hear of a second marriage, however, since that would mean forfeiting the usufruct on Saskia's property. There are indications that Saskia's uncle Hendrick Uylenburg, a respectable Mennonite, was furious – and all this at a time when Rembrandt's relations with the royal court were cooling. The stream of portrait commissions dried up from one day to the next.

Five years later, twenty-year-old Hendrickje Stoffels came to work in the Rembrandt household as a maid. According to Houbraken she was a peasant girl, 'rather small in her person, but a well-made creature, and plump of body'. Complications were inevitable, and in 1649 Geertje Dircx left the house on the Breestraat. An unsavoury lawsuit followed: Rembrandt had agreed to pay Geertje sixty guilders a year as a maintenance allowance, but she regarded that as far too little. After a tempestuous scene in Rembrandt's kitchen she summoned him to appear before the Commissioners of Matrimonial Affairs for breach of promise. A marriage was not on the cards because of their difference in station, as she was well aware, but she was able to get the stipend raised to two hundred guilders a year. Her demand was recorded in the Marital Disputes Book kept by the city authorities: 'The defendant denies having made promises of marriage to the plaintiff but states that he is under no obligation to admit to having slept with her, stating that it is for the plaintiff to prove the same.' Rembrandt then hit back. Along with her brother and cousin, who came to collect the stipend, he managed to bribe a certain Cornelia Jansdochter to take statements from other neighbourhood women about Geertje's conduct. On that basis the trio had Geertje Dircx locked up in the Spinhuis in Gouda, a house of correction and madhouse combined. She was not released until 1655, after several of her friends intervened.

A new scandal followed in 1654, when Hendrickje Stoffels became pregnant and was sent for by the consistory of the Reformed Church on the grounds that, as a document recovered later puts it, she 'was guilty of whoring with Rembrandt the painter'. The painter himself got off scot free. He was not a member of the Church, so the clergy had nothing to say about him. Yet he could have spared himself a great deal of social misery had he married Hendrickje Stoffels. It seems likely that the only reason he decided not to do so was lack of money. After all, if he married again, he would have to give Saskia's inheritance to his son Titus, and he no longer had any way of raising the twenty thousand guilders.

This meant that Rembrandt had broken a second code of

the Amsterdam elite: financial solvency. He had discovered a rather curious means of financing his lavish lifestyle. His work was so sought-after for so long that his clients were happy to lend him money, in order to have at least a moral claim that might perhaps ensure he actually completed the work. There even emerged a small market in Rembrandt IOUs of this kind – somewhat speculative, of course, since no one knew whether or not the master would ever actually produce the promised painting.

In about 1654 the scheme started to backfire. Rembrandt could not honour all his old promises and he was no longer receiving new loans because this was a period in which every merchant kept a tight hand on the purse strings. Holland was at war with England, most ships were unable to reach the city, unemployment and bankruptcy threatened, and Amsterdammers suddenly realized just how vulnerable their economy was.

In December 1655, Rembrandt held a sale of paintings and other possessions in the Keizerskroon Inn on the Kalverstraat. It raised little money. Six months later he was forced to file for bankruptcy and the Desolate Boedelskamer at the town hall took charge of proceedings from then on. One of the creditors who caused considerable trouble, as is clear from the bankruptcy application, was Geertje Dircx, since released from the Spinhuis in Gouda. She even threatened to have him imprisoned for debt if he did not come up with the two hundred guilder stipend to which she was entitled. But shortly afterwards she died.

Again Rembrandt was confronted with the power of the clergy. In cases of financial insolvency the consistory of the Amsterdam Reformed Church played the role of moral judge.

Was this an honest merchant who had fallen on hard times or could he be accused of cunning and guile? Had efforts been made to repair the damage, or had items actually been removed from the estate? In the former case there was talk of insolvency, in the latter of bankruptcy – unacceptable in this Calvinist city.

Rembrandt, as all the documents make clear, used every trick in the book to keep as much of his property as possible out of the bankruptcy proceedings. First he tried to secure the house on the Breestraat by transferring ownership to his son Titus. Later he formally became an employee of Titus and Hendrickje, so that he could no longer be called upon by his creditors to repay the money he owed. Officially he had nothing to do with the clergy, but socially all this tampering saw him branded a bankrupt. No Six would want to have his bride painted by such a man.

The house on the Breestraat was sold, the furniture went to the pawnbroker's on the Oudezijds Voorburgwal (a building that still stands) to be sold there. Titus, still only seventeen, managed to use his savings to buy back, at one of the furniture sales, the valuable ebony-framed mirror that his father had used to paint his self-portraits. But as it was being carried home it was shattered.

Rembrandt's last works took on a different tone from his earlier pieces. The outlines became indistinct, foreground and background merged, rooms grew vague and dissolved into infinity.

The biggest commission on offer in those years, the decoration of the interior of the new town hall, had gone to Govert Flinck. When Flinck died prematurely, Rembrandt was allowed to take over only one small part of the commission: the conspiracy of Claudius Civilis. By 1662 his huge canvas had been removed on the orders of the great and the good, and the work was completed by a less famous painter, based on the sketch by Govert Flinck.

Rembrandt had meanwhile moved to the Rozengracht. He retained the support of only a few members of the Amsterdam elite, among them the arms dealer Jacob Trip. In the year that he drew Elsje Christiaens, abject poverty forced him to sell Saskia's grave in the Oude Kerk. At that time, epidemics of plague raged through the city at regular intervals, and in areas like the Jordaan in particular there might be thousands of victims in just a few weeks. 'In the Bloemstraat there were twenty-seven dead the day before yesterday, today there are twenty-two in the Anjeliersstraat, and yesterday in the Barndesteeg three from a single house were buried,' a woman called Magdalena Stockmans wrote in a letter to a friend during an epidemic of bubonic plague in the summer of 1655.

A 'pale flame of fire' fell from the heavens one evening that year, at half past ten, as if 'a burning torch was dropping out of the sky'. A few months later a fiery ball appeared in the sky above Amsterdam, radiating short fat beams and 'giving a very pale yet clear light, in the form of flames', as eighteenth-century Amsterdam historian Jan Wagenaar described it. In 1663-4 more than thirty thousand died of the plague – one in seven Amsterdammers. They included 'plump of body' Hendrickje Stoffels. Five years later Titus died, aged twenty-seven and recently married. A year after that, Rembrandt himself met his end. He was buried on 4 October 1669 in an unmarked, rented grave in the Westerkerk.

When the church was renovated three hundred years later,

it was thought for a moment that his grave had been found. The body was uncovered and the skull crumbled to dust with the cameras of the national evening news trained on it. As it turned out, it was not the master after all.

Making tracks around the Central Station

Not until the dawn slowly started to colour the sky above the IJ did the world behind the Central Station come to an end. Most of the girls were still standing there, and from time to time they cadged a cigarette from us, but it was starting to wind up, you could tell.

'Come on, you bug-eyed tossers,' Hilga from The Hague was shouting at the Opels, Volvos and BMWs that kept driving straight past. 'It's going well, really well,' Astrid whispered as she walked by after her seventh client. 'Know what? Tommy and I are going to live together. We're getting a room. Together. In Het Hekeltje.'

Hilga meanwhile, with her short dumpy body, her boxer's face, the sweater that barely reached down over her crotch and her bare legs ravaged by life and the weather, had started walking down the middle of the road. She hadn't had a client all night. 'Come and get it guys. Or do I have to take my knickers off as well?'

On the benches close to the edge of the IJ, Jan and Marten were asleep – a few rags and some bits of cardboard with the occasional arm or leg sticking out. Down by the water were a few unknowns, bottles of fruit wine next to them. On the loading platform right beside the station's middle entrance, Tommy was sitting drinking lager with some Belgian guy. As for Rick and me, we were going to make sure Gina got away safely. Gina, who can howl like a hurricane, who takes on half the canal with her whoring, pilfering and scrounging, and who then hangs on your arm, jumping up and down and chattering like a schoolgirl.

It had been a remarkable night, one of those long May nights on which Rick and I roamed the city together, Rick because he had no choice – he was a man of no fixed abode, had been for years – while I was a sort of privileged hanger-on.

First we'd loitered for a bit in the warmth of the Central Station. As on every other night, the six telephone boxes by the main entrance were in continual use from about midnight onwards. Anyone who'd scored a bit of heroin would go and stand in one of them to smoke or inject it. We'd run into Gina and Jan there. 'Leave us alone for a bit, Rickie, can't you see we're busy.' We'd also seen a girl who at first sight looked neatly dressed. As soon as she got into the phone box she did a little conjuring trick with a lighter, discreetly raised her skirt a fraction and expertly sank the needle into her thigh.

In the almost empty station concourse we'd stood for a while to watch the last of the passengers hurry through while the floor-cleaning machines were already hard at it. Leaning against the pillars and walls were fifteen or so Moroccan vagrants, some of them still barely into adolescence, and an older man sauntering among them. It was a wordless affair, out there on the tiles of that vast hall, a kind of chess game of glances and tiny gestures. But suddenly the man went up to one of the boys and within seconds the concourse was minus two chess pieces.

'They're cheap, those boys', I heard later. Twenty-five guilders for a whole night at it, with perhaps two or three hours' sleep, breakfast and then back out on the street. But at least you'd have a roof over your head for a few hours. 'You can make more than that, but only if you're very young. Maybe double if you've only just run away.'

Later we bumped into Hilga from The Hague again, crouching down to search under a couple of loose tiles. 'God, I feel terrible,' she said. 'Guys, this is really bad, I'm starting to crash. Jesus Christ.' There was a time when 'the doctor' sometimes hid his supply of wraps there – no dealer walks around with his entire stock on him – so it was her last hope.

At night the area known as the Wallen was the centre of the action. Men urinated in the street, shouting at each other, and as the evening wore on a sticky layer of foot sweat and stale beer formed in the canal and on the pavement. Around three there was a muddled fight between two dealers on the German bridge; a lot of yelling in Sranantongo. One of them produced a knife, but when three cops rushed him he flung it under a car. As soon as the knife wielder was handcuffed, his opponent leapt at him with the discarded blade, and it would all have ended in a bloody mess if a policewoman hadn't thrown herself between them, blonde hair flying.

Then suddenly there was Gina, in excellent spirits. She'd got hold of a full six wraps. One was for her boyfriend Tall Jan, and the rest she was putting aside for a while. 'Why don't you walk a little way with me,' she said. On Rick's arm she chatted nineteen to the dozen. About the mild weather, about some idiot who'd put something in her beer a few days ago that made her so completely crazy she'd even attacked her own Jan. 'They pulled that one on Klaas with the Ponytail later too. When he got home everything was moving and there were black Surinamers coming out of the wallpaper everywhere.'

Her voice resounded across the silent Warmoesstraat. We ran into some dealers who started cursing her. 'Fucking bitch!' 'Lousy cunt!' She held forth on the subject of a tetanus injection she'd been given that had made her have two periods, one immediately after the other. 'That's exactly what's meant to happen. In women the dirty blood always flows out of the body via the cunt. I don't know how it works with men. Do you know, Rick?'

While we were standing waiting for the ferry she started to get worried. Would Jan be there waiting for her? 'Ricky,' she kept asking. 'What do you think? Will he still be there?'

On our way back, in the first light of morning, we happened to run into Hilga again.

'Got something after all,' she called to us from a distance. 'A drunk. Gave him a quickie down there by the station cycle racks. Took fifteen minutes. He was pretty incapable but all the same: two twenty-fives!'

Now it's fully light. 'Come on, let's make tracks,' says Rick and we keep walking. We scrounge a roll-up, get hold of a beer and set off again. When you first arrive in this city you're homeless, and if you're homeless there are only a few places you can go. Everywhere else needs paying for. So it's a matter of walking, sitting, hanging around, waiting without anything to wait for, and then walking again, since you have to do something.

Almost everyone on the street has a past – drink, drugs, a divorce, trouble with the law. Some are fresh out of psychiatric institutions, others are in the country illegally and simply don't exist for the rest of society. If you're not very careful, then once you're on the street you quickly find yourself in a cycle of pennilessness and filth that ends in one form of beggary or another. Then it's almost impossible to escape, because no employer or landlord will ever accept you in that condition.

The Legion of Dishonour has several thousand men and a hundred or so women to its name in this city, but the professors have been arguing over the precise numbers for years. Down the ages they've included only a handful of women. Almost all are men. 'Every woman has a you-know-what, an eternal money-maker, and things have to get pretty weird before she stops being able to pay for a roof over her head with it,' the boys say, jealous.

Rick is a smallish, nondescript, black-haired man with a narrow face and a dash of Indonesian blood in his veins. I know him from a former life. Things didn't go well, but even on the street he's still the odd man out. He used to be a social worker. He has two divorces behind him, was thrown out of the house and hit rock bottom, then to cap it all he fell ill. He told me the whole story one rainy afternoon as we were standing on the Albert Cuypstraat waiting for the market to close, describing the inevitable downward spiral you end up in once you find yourself on the street. 'Your first instinct is to go to a big city,' he said. 'There are so many more opportunities to find food there, and more places where you'll be left alone.'

After that, however, or so I gather from Rick's stories, a rather Kafkaesque situation develops. For the first few months – and in some cases this can last for one or two years – you receive no state benefits as a homeless person because you have no fixed abode. Conversely, you can't get a room or anywhere else to live because you don't have any money. 'So you're completely stuck. And you go downhill rapidly from there.'

The benefits problem can sometimes be tackled by means of a postal address, a place where you live for officialdom's sake. It might be a charitable organization, but it could also be the address of a commercial guesthouse, a bar or a gambling den. You usually have to pay serious money for one, sometimes hundreds of guilders a month, and charity workers will often impose all kinds of conditions that don't appeal to most young people.

In this city you can survive reasonably well without money. As we sat talking, the time approached five and the stallholders began dismantling their stalls, a process that involved a great deal of clattering and banging. Before our eyes an alternative kind of shopping scene emerged. Blemished oranges, over-ripe mangos, split red peppers or cucumbers – they were all rapidly thrust into plastic bags by casual passers-by. Before long there were at least fifty people hunting through the piles of rubbish behind the stalls. It happened swiftly and efficiently. They'd all obviously done this before, and they all knew they'd have to be quick otherwise the stallholders would start shouting and cursing.

A couple of well-dressed mothers with children were beavering away behind an orange stall. An elderly man found a bunch of brownish bananas on the street, and a little further on a skinny, half-naked boy in short trousers was eating raw fish out of a plastic waste barrel. On a street corner a small, secretive exchange market started up. 'I've got two cauliflowers to spare. Anyone have any fruit?'

The garbage-pickers sweep through the market in waves every day, I'm told. It starts at half past four with a few young women and some elderly people, the types who are least likely to be chased away. Then at five o'clock the ordinary homeless or semi-homeless spread out across the market. The last group doesn't emerge until after half past five, people so dirty and unkempt that they'd be shooed off immediately if the stallholders were still around. They arrive at the market at the last possible moment, more or less following on behind the garbage trucks, slouching in their rags, sometimes barefoot.

For anyone hungry enough, the city has several other places where food is available. In the first weeks of winter, doughnut stalls are set up at various places in the town centre to sell the traditional *oliebollen*. Near to closing time a large plastic sack full of unsold stock appears on the street and before long you'll see shadows dash towards it. Then there are the Augustine nuns in the Warmoesstraat, who dole out bags of bread. A particular favourite is Mother Theresa in the Egelantiersstraat. Every day at a quarter to four and again at four thirty, long lines of men, and a few women, gather at the door. Inside, in a large bare dining room with long tables, some two hundred impoverished Dutch people are served a meal by a handful of Indian nuns. They perform the task with humility and not the slightest hint of condescension, which I suspect is the main reason they're so popular, even among young people who want nothing to do with the ministrations of other charitable groups. During the prayer at the start of the meal almost all of us murmur along to the words, our eyes firmly shut, in our frayed jackets or old coats, perhaps wrapped in a blanket: 'Holy Mary, Mother of God, pray for us sinners, now and in the hour of our death.'

At Mother Theresa the quality of the food very much depends on what the nuns have been able to wheedle out of Amsterdam shops and catering firms. Some days suddenly everyone gets a hamburger or meat with salad, but there are times when it's only bread and a thin soup on offer. On the occasions when Rick and I ate there, it was usually something in between, a kind of thick broth made of root vegetables, with bits of sausage in it.

One time we were given a huge chunk of currant loaf, containing raisins and nuts as well as currants. 'Expensive currant loaf; good currant loaf,' the man sitting opposite us muttered, and the conversation soon turned to the quality of the other eating establishments used by those at the bottom of the social scale. At Hare Krishna you can eat for free every day, but it's always the same, my fellow diners complained: 'Rice with bits of cauliflower, carrots and curry sauce.' The Salvation Army has meals out of the freezer, but you almost always have to pay. By far the best dinners are served once a month by a pastor on the Wallen, everyone agreed about that. 'You always eat well there, three courses, and you get a bag of oranges too, and a tube of peppermints,' the man across from us said. 'But first you have to sit through a church service, in which his daughter plays guitar.'

'You promised me something,' Gina shouted out from the other side of the water one afternoon. 'I didn't promise you anything,' said Rick. 'Yes you did, as soon as you got a bit of a break. Come on Rick, five guilders.' 'But I've just seen Jan with two tenners, enough to pack up and go home.' 'I'm not with Jan any more. I don't care what Jan does, I don't give a rat's arse.' 'I've heard that one before.' 'There's nothing between me and Jan any more, it's just that he keeps bugging me. Soon as I step onto the bridge he wants a can of beer. Okay fine, beer down his gullet, whop, gone. But then he needs another. I'm sick to death of it. Want a swig, Rick?' From the distance we hear Jan's whimpering voice coming closer, 'Did Rick come to the party?' 'You're a liar,' said Gina. 'What do you mean liar?' 'Rick saw you with something to trade this afternoon, in the Bijenkorf.' 'That wasn't mine, that make-up box. I sold it for that girl. Aren't I allowed to luck out for a twenty-five? You shouldn't talk about things you know nothing about.' 'You're lying, you bullshitter,' Gina shouts. 'You went bragging to Ricky that it was your deal.' Jan turns to Rick: 'Don't you have two guilders for me, Rick?' Rick shakes his head. Jan says to Gina: 'He's got something alright otherwise he wouldn't have joined the parade.' Gina says: 'Gone is gone. His money's gone. Must have drunk it. So it's gone.'

The world is small and in this circuit everyone knows everyone else. There's old Jan, Gina's Tall Jan who spends three nights a week in a police cell and has just served six months for a stabbing. There's Rick, universally known as Glimpie. There's Dirty Tom who can't keep his hands off little girls and who calls himself the Council Superintendant of all children's playgrounds, and Simon Swig, who features on all the Salvation Army posters at the Central Station, with his grey beard, captioned: 'We believe. But not in "sort it out for yourself".' In the photo, instead of his eternal can of lager, he's holding a plastic cup of coffee – something the lads on the street describe as a unique sight. Simon, coffee and bread hadn't been seen together since he was a little boy. As for Simon himself, he grumbles about the scandalous misuse that has been made of his face, but among the beer drinkers on the benches at the Amstelveld and the Nieuwmarkt, the wildest stories are doing the rounds about how much he was paid for his compliance. The truth no doubt lies somewhere in between.

Rick offers the following assessment of his fellow homeless. First there are people who make a 'voluntary' decision to become vagrants. They exist, although he believes there are very few of them. The second category constitutes some thirty per cent of the total: former or current psychiatric patients. The rest vary greatly depending how long they've been living on the street. They progress, as it were, from category one to category two. 'The first few months you wander aimlessly through the city in search of, well, of a new footing,' Rick says. 'But after about a year, life on the street starts to shake you apart. If you weren't an alcoholic to begin with you become one, if only to drive off the cold at night. Those who were already drinking become rubbish bins. They start to consume all the things God has forbidden, drink, drugs, sleeping pills, pep pills, whatever they can lay their hands on, preferably all at the same time.'

The ultimate result? Some are picked up off the street by the council and eventually find themselves in psychiatric institutions. A great many are rejected completely by the rest of humanity, drink all the welfare money they receive and continue to live rough most of the time. Then there are those who put an end to it all. In cold winters especially, quite a few people have been known to walk into the IJ or one of the canals – 'gone swimming', as it's known on the street.

By chance I once witnessed the outcome of such an event, on a wet January evening in the Kloveniersburgwal. There wasn't a great deal to see. At the edge of the canal a little group of people stood talking, the police were in attendance, two divers were swimming around in the water and a little later they dragged out a shapeless body. I heard that a girl had suddenly stood up in a bar, walked outside, and without a moment's hesitation threw herself into the icy water. 'Some stupid whore,' the men said.

Walking, sitting, rolling a cigarette, waiting for nothing, and then the stories. Everyone has his own legend. Everyone is a hero in his own jungle.

One Sunday morning, Rick and I sat with some fifteen others on a bridge near the Keizersgracht, drinking beer. On Sundays everyone is always on the street. The homeless shelters are shut then, whether it's sunny, raining, snowing or hailing – that's simply the way it works. But this Sunday the weather was glorious, and everyone had come to the area around the Utrechtsestraat where there's a Jewish delicatessen, the only place in the city where you can buy cheap half-litre bottles of Heineken at ten o'clock on a Sunday morning. The sun was shining, the bells were ringing, one bottle after another was opened and I noticed for the first time that some of the young men in the group could drink so quickly that their throats didn't move, they literally poured the beer down.

The conversation turned to old age. 'Eat plenty of beans. You'll live to be a hundred that way, on beans and gravy.' They moved on to the subject of someone they knew who had liver trouble and 'had to switch to chocolate milk', and then on to everything that made life exciting and interesting.

'That's impossible, Rick,' Gina says. 'You can never turn a woman into a man. If a woman has a cunt, there's no way you can make a prick out of it, with a pair of balls. That's impossible, right?' After pausing a moment she goes on: 'You can turn a man into a woman. A man has a cock...' 'Really?' Rick grins. 'Right, so they stick that over towards the back and make a split in it and then you get a cunt. But not a woman into a man, that's impossible, I've never heard of it.'

Somewhere else in the group they're discussing the possibility of spending the weeks of the Soccer World Cup in jail, so as to watch television undisturbed. Almost everyone on the street owes a couple of days for some petty crime or other. A man they call grandpa instructs them. 'You just go to a phone box and ring the police and say there's a weird guy on the street waving and shouting, and then you only need to go and stand there and when they see your twisted visage they're bound to take you with them.'

In the course of the morning the mood of the group changes like the hands of a clock, slowly but relentlessly. There is talk of death. In my notes I read: Manus: 'Jan-Willem's dead.' Henk: 'God. Fuck. So that's a funeral I'll have to go to.' Manus: 'Smashed himself up in a car, yesterday.' Rick: 'Good thing I didn't get in it with him.' 'Burial next Tuesday. Forty-three, he was.' 'Think how stupid that makes him, stepping off so soon.' 'He's still my brother, though.' 'Crashed into someone else, too. He'll probably end up in a wheelchair.' Henk: 'I don't think Jan-Willem even had a driver's license. He just drove anyway, olé, yo-ho hey hey!' 'A good death all the same. Not that you'd wish it on anyone, but if you smash yourself up then at least you're gone in a flash.'

Jan-Willem, meanwhile, is ten metres behind us, calmly sitting chatting on a bench with old Simon Swig.

In the hours that follow, peace gradually ebbs away. Rick is abruptly hit with a bottle by Arie, and the others have to intervene to calm things down. Then there's a great flurry of activity, a bit of walking, half a bag of chips someone found somewhere and then, suddenly, another day is over.

Who in this group really does live on the street, day and night, and who doesn't? Is there nothing left at all of a previous life? It's never really clear. In the world of the street, people come and go all the time. Very often guys will sleep on the street for a few months, manage to find shelter with a friend or acquaintance for a while then resort to the street again. They may have a spell in hospital, or even get a room for a bit, before ending up on the street again and so it goes on.

In the official shelters for the homeless you're only ever allowed to stay for about four days, so there are people who trail from city to city, hopping from one shelter to the next, as it were. It's a very old trick. George Orwell and Charles Dickens described it, and it's been taken up by generations of vagrants all over the world. Except that in this country you don't hitch a ride or walk but travel comfortably by train. Without paying, of course. A filthy appearance often has a sufficiently intimidating effect on the conductors, and anyhow a night in the cells means another night's shelter, plus breakfast. Most of the homeless I met were nevertheless remarkably reluctant to wander. 'At least you know all the guys around here.'

Within the city there are several different homelessness circuits: illegals, youngsters, youth gangs in the suburbs, junkies, North Africans, Italians, Brits, rent boys – all of them closed groups that live more or less separately from each other. There's even a certain animosity between the drug users and the alcoholics. Druggies think the Heineken types are old fools, while the alkies see the junkies as spoilt babies who have everything organized for them, whereas a normal tramp has little to fall back on, aside from a few charities. 'If you're on junk there's any number of places you can go, to sleep, get free food, all kinds of things, simply because you're so much trouble and so pathetic,' a non-drug-user grumbled to me one evening when one junkie squabble after another had resounded down the street. 'If you can manage to sniff or shoot up two to three hundred guilders a day, then I'm sorry, but you can buy bread and spend seven or eight guilders on a cheap bed for the night. If you drink or inject that much money, then I don't have any sympathy. It's your own damn fault.'

Codes of honour are few, but they undoubtedly exist. There's a great deal of scrounging, but you always need to do something in return. Snitching is taboo. Old Martin, who borrowed too much and gave nothing back, left for another city for a while to be on the safe side, and when someone from 'my' group was handed a twenty-five to fetch a crate of beer and didn't come back, he was given a good beating the following day.

The worst punishment, however, is rather different. A dip in the canal. Because if you're sleeping on the street, the main enemy isn't pain or cold but damp.

I saw it one time. A North African had found a sleeping place in an empty boat on the Wallen that turned out to belong to someone else. While a couple of fellow indigents stood on the bridge cheering, the man was suspended from the edge in total panic, half in the water, his brown-speckled buttocks almost bare. A little later he was chased further away by the group, soaking wet, squealing and howling with fear, shouting in a language no one could understand.

Let's make no bones about it: anyone living on the street commits a multitude of sins. There's the drinking, swearing and fighting, sometimes a spell of shoplifting at the Bijenkorf department store, and the way the two sexes treat each other is not always as it should be. Even though these are childish pranks compared to what happens in the rest of the city, it's amazing how many Christian institutions suddenly start accosting you if you hang about on the bottom rungs of society. As soon as we've shaken off the folders from one street mission, the next little choir is ready and waiting.

One time Rick and I started the night at a coffee bar run by 'Youth with a Mission'. The first cup of coffee is free and you can sit comfortably in the warm for a while. Among the guests were quite a few people we knew from the circuit. Across from us a large black man lay sleeping, head on his enormous hands. Now and then, befuddled, he would adjust his position, shake his head a few times like a wet mop, and then carry on sleeping.

Gospel music was playing in the background, and as it began to get dark, more and more nicely dressed young people with happy smiling faces came in and distributed themselves between our tables. 'But aren't you afraid of the life after this life?' we heard an earnest young man say to an old tramp who was leaning against a wall with trembling hands and bloodshot eyes. 'Hell, I mean?'

We watched a very beautiful, blonde, innocent girl bravely start up a conversation with Dirty Tommy – for those with any idea of Tommy's main field of interest a rather comical sight. Later she approached us. She said she was eighteen and from Norway, and in mildly purple prose she went on to describe the joys of heaven. 'Sometimes I want to die now, already, so I can be there, with Jesus,' she said.

We'd barely got outside, or to the German bridge, which is usually teeming with prostitutes, when we were stopped by a choir singing 'Hosanna' in English, accompanied by several guitars. Next to them stood a small group of Baptists and a few metres further on an older man buttonholed us: 'We're from Youth with a Mission. But Jesus is Lord of Us All, it doesn't matter which church. The question is, do you have a relationship with him? That's the crucial thing.' Rick told him: 'I've got a relationship with myself, which is far more important.' To which the man replied: 'The choice is up to you, Jesus or the outer darkness.' For poor fag-end grubbers like Rick and his friends there was no escaping them.

I have to say something about the short-lived romance between Angela and Troll. They must once have come from somewhere in the east, in their old van. They were intending to travel all around the world, but the engine soon gave out and here they were. Angela earned a living streetwalking behind the Central Station and Troll did various kinds of odd jobs in demolition. Angela was small and skinny. Troll looked the way you'd expect from his name, and when his big hairy body appeared in the doorway of his van, the whole vehicle would tilt wildly to one side.

First they stayed near the docks; later the council moved their van to a bare windy terrain set aside for caravans, campers and the homeless, between oil storage tanks and a breaker's yard, somewhere halfway to the coast, a place where you drive off the map and disappear into an indeterminate world of brown and green.

Yet despite the cold, rain, mud and overcrowding, there

of all places a new era began for Angela and Troll. Through a kind-hearted social worker, Angela got herself appointed official cleaner of the toilet trailers. By taking her on, the city struck gold, since it turned out that somewhere in Angela's skinny body lurked a profoundly German, housewifely sense of cleanliness. Never were the toilets as sparkling as in those happy months. Meanwhile Troll specialized in the unblocking of toilets – in such circles the toilet paper is usually gone within an hour, after which people switch to using sanitary towels, underpants, old T-shirts and other problematic materials – and so the council saved itself many thousands of guilders in plumber's fees over the weeks that followed. '*Das machen wir doch so!*' he would announce almost every morning, before sticking his long arm down into a stinking toilet bowl again.

There were other enclaves of that kind in the city for those with nowhere else to live: settlements of huts, tents, sometimes old caravans. Leefland, for example, an idyllic area between a scattering of gasometers and the harbour; it was almost like the dunes. Then there was the stretch of wasteland near Slotervaart Station, or, closer to the city centre, an undeveloped area behind some offices and a building supplies store, again near the docks.

We once went to visit a lonely Afghan in Leefland. Next to his caravan he'd built a kind of tea house on the sand, an open-air living room complete with a carpet, a television, a table with a vase of flowers on it, and an upside-down map of the Netherlands on the wall. A few hundred metres further along a Spaniard lived in an old, unbelievably dirty council toilet trailer. A few months later the trailer was 'sold on' by the Spaniard to three North Africans, who cleaned it, put down some proper vinyl flooring and magically transformed the whole thing into an alternative maisonette. On the same land lived several dozen more young North African men who had some five caravans between them. They took turns sleeping in them, crammed together, as shift-sleepers. They lived on vice and air. Every evening they left, neatly spruced up, for the Central Station or some nightclub or other, but when Ramadan ended they put together a meal on home-made tables outdoors that their neighbours never stopped talking about.

Right now the council is trying to get rid of them all. The terrain is being cleared and most of the huts and caravans incinerated. The residents are leaving for other places or reverting to sleeping in doorways and under bridges with other street boys and street girls.

Things eventually soured between Angela and Troll. After several happy weeks the neighbours would sometimes see Angela storming off on her stiletto heels, all the way past the wrecked cars to the bus stop, with Troll panting along behind her on his transport bicycle. In the distance they would stop and talk, before eventually riding back together on that one bicycle. But in the early spring there came a day when they didn't turn back.

The latest news is that Angela is working at a sex club in Coevorden, and no one has ever heard anything more from Troll.

At half past eight on a Tuesday morning, on the Kloveniersburgwal, I saw a naked woman on the street for the first time, outside the door to number 84. A wet, cold mist filled the air and she was changing her clothes. Her old clothing was heaped up on the pavement and she was fishing something new out of a rubbish bag. She was perhaps about thirty-five, and the red of her hands and face contrasted with the whiteness of the rest of her body. She wasn't skinny, but neither was she fat. Her hair hung loose down her back, just above her buttocks she had little dimples, and for all their fragility her tiny feet were planted firmly on the wet paving stones, as relaxed as if the city was her bedroom.

Dozens of people walked past, on their way to work or to school, and not one of them gave her so much as a passing glance.

Anybody finding themselves on their uppers can simply sleep on the street – or in a hollow with a few planks on top as they do on the undeveloped land at the edge of the city – but there are other options too. Under the bridges near the National Maritime Museum, for instance, or in an old goods wagon on the Rietlanden. For years you could take a short illegal walk through the metro tunnel and find a place to sleep in the niches under the platforms of the Wibautstraat station, but that opportunity is now closed off. You can find excellent sleeping places in North, I learned from Rick, in storage yards or in the bushes near the tunnel under the IJ. The Sarphatipark is also popular at the moment.

No normal person would sleep at the Salvation Army, or not often anyhow, the guys tell me. A bed there costs about eight guilders, but because it's used mainly by addicts, you're unlikely to get an undisturbed night's sleep. According to Rick, 'at four o'clock the first of the junkies starts prowling about because the dope has worn off, and at five the second one wakes up and they start griping to each other about how long they'll have to wait before they can get their methadone'. Any normal young man prefers to sleep under a bridge, he says.

There are two private hostels for the homeless, Het Hekeltje and De Drie Paardjes, but no one recommends those either. For years conditions at both were downright nineteenth century: dirt, fire hazard, soaking wet walls, mouldy beds. Vagrants could stay there only if they signed a document stating that their welfare payments were to be paid directly into the owner's bank account. The owner of De Drie Paardjes and her son conducted a veritable reign of terror over the men living there. They were given pocket money only if they behaved themselves. Foreigners were forced to hand over their passports to the woman, which made them totally dependent on her. A few years ago both hostels were closed down, but after refurbishment they opened again and according to the homeless people I spoke to, the owners have since resumed their lucrative withholding practices on the same terms as before.

One night Rick and I were sitting under a tree on the Jonas Daniël Meijerplein. It was one o'clock in the morning. A light rain was falling and the drops were trickling down between the leaves. This was not a good place to sleep, since the wet, as Rick had made very clear to me early on, is worse for the homeless than gales, cold, or anything else the weather can throw at you. You can't freeze to death in this city, but all other causes of death are open to you. When there's a really hard frost, all kinds of establishments open up for the night, but as long as it only rains, snows or hails, the council won't lift a finger to help.

We had to get moving. On nights like this you're best off

under the Schellingwoude Bridge, or behind the Central Station, or in Overtoomse Veld, where there's a church with all kinds of nooks and crannies. So we walked around looking, while the rain slowly but surely soaked us to the skin. As we walked, Rick gave me a lecture on homelessness skills. Many young men do without a sleeping bag, he tells me, even when it's extremely cold. That's stupid, but given their nature and their way of living it's not hard to understand. Apart from a sleeping bag, the best remedy for the cold is the bottle. You knock back the contents as fast as you can and then you'll sleep for a few hours. You inevitably wake up after that, usually shivering. You have to get up and walk about for a bit, jump up and down to get the blood flowing again. From that point on you won't sleep any more.

We hadn't reached that stage yet. We decided to go to Help for the Homeless where, as so-called 'transients', we had a right to shelter for a maximum of four nights per month. You're treated well there and the only drawback is that after four days – barring exceptional circumstances – they inevitably show you the door.

We trudged to Overtoomse Veld.

The building is called De Veste, the fortress, and when we rang the bell the door opened only a crack. Apart from the men on the door and the social worker, just about everyone seemed to be walking around in a long white shirt that reached to their ankles. That's how they do things at Help for the Homeless. As soon as you come in you have to hand over everything, remove all your clothes and take a shower. Your clothing can then be washed immediately overnight.

There was a doctor, too. On the evening I spoke to him he'd seen three people with alcohol and withdrawal problems, a man who turned out to have serious alcohol-related liver damage, two frightened and feverish illegals, an exceptionally confused woman and a man who kept following him around, with a large scar on his naked belly.

The number of former psychiatric patients wandering the streets was increasing rapidly, as far as the doctor could see. The consequences of budget cuts at psychiatric institutions in far-off forests were more and more in evidence under the bridges of the city. 'They're people who've given up trying to get anywhere; the saddest group of all, really.' He said they did sometimes come to De Veste, but often you'd see them simply wandering around town, with ropes of totally filthy hair, finding something in a rubbish bin here and there.

He was a calm, committed man, that vagrant-doctor. He'd worked in a developing country before taking a job in this city. He told me that the reality of the lives of the homeless astonished him time and again. They nearly all seemed far older than they actually were. Life on the street grinds you down.

This is compounded by the fact that access to doctors and hospitals is often difficult. When your entire existence is stored in a plastic bag, your state health insurance card may sometimes get lost, if you have one at all.

Then there's the cold. During harsh winters he'd sometimes seen people with frostbitten limbs. But that wasn't the most important thing, the doctor believed. It was the vagrant life as a whole that meant people could no longer care for themselves. 'You hear stories of truly miserable lives,' the doctor said, 'because in this city you won't end up on the street for some trivial reason. Usually a great deal has happened before you reach that stage.'

He believed that being homeless meant far more than not

having a house. It was mainly a matter of being without any kind of social network, which also explains why, apart from a few cases of sheer bad luck, it mainly affects people in three specific groups: new arrivals (almost all of them teenagers or illegal immigrants), the mentally disturbed, and those who, because of addiction for example, have behaved in such a way that they are outcasts from their entire social environment. As the doctor put it, 'When someone ends up on the street, it's often only then that it finally gets through to them: now I really am homeless. But by then it's usually too late. By that time all the doors, whether of friends, acquaintances or relatives, are firmly shut.'

One evening we had some money, and in Emmelot, a bar on a corner by the German bridge, we ran into Carlo and Regina. Regina was a beautiful girl with a full figure and a strong German accent. Carlo had done some kind of work in clubs and the sex trade and he was just spending a bit of time abroad to avoid tax. Regina had stood on the German bridge for years. Carlo had dragged her out of that life and now they were living together in Regina's native village in Germany – happily ever after, they said.

The conversation quickly turned to the subject of the increasing depravity in the red-light district. 'The atmosphere is really not good anymore,' Carlo felt. He complained that the girls looked bad and that they often worked for less than they should. 'Two or three years ago they still had style,' he said. 'But now, well now you can get a blow job for ten guilders in the corner of a doorway.' Regina added: 'I've earned so much cash, it's incredible. We worked it out a while ago. I shot 3.6 million into my arms in twelve years.'

She learned the tricks from the other girls. 'I rarely actually had to give anyone a blow job. You just spit on your hand, hold the business end to your neck and move firmly along it, and he'll pay, a good bit, too. Screwing – same thing: spit between your thighs. It's a skilled job. You need to become expert at it. Think about when a girl has her period. If you didn't pull a few tricks you wouldn't earn anything. You learn how.'

She believed the market had been ruined by runaways and foreign girls. 'They screwed men for real in their cars. And the guys noticed of course. Huh? Doesn't feel at all like it does with the women on the dyke. So then they wanted the same from us.

'Just look at the men standing here on the bridge. All older men, divorced men, men whose wives have died – all poor and lonely no doubt, but they're also the most perverse and filthy characters I know. They take a girl with them for the night, give her a roof over her head and perhaps a bit of breakfast and a T-shirt, say, and then they ask for something in return...' Carlo says: 'I know men who only go for that kind of girl, the lonely ones, the runaways. They seek them out.'

'AIDS doesn't interest you if you're sick, if you have goose bumps, if you're illegal,' Regina tells me. 'Try to imagine. You get fifty guilders for normal. But if you screw without a rubber you get a hundred. For a hundred guilders you can buy two shots. That means you can pretty soon go home and get to lie down in the peace and quiet at last, in your own warm bed, with your own fella, or simply alone, away from all those pigs who want to be pissed on and spat at or to put their fist up your arse, because they think they can do all that with a junkie prostitute...'

Outside there's suddenly a huge shouting match, 'Filthy

whore!' 'Fuck you!' 'Let go of that man, leave him alone.' 'Come on, let's go have a nice little sit in my room.' 'Leave that man alone!' 'Filthy bitch!'

We rush out onto the street. It looks like an ordinary quarrel, but to anyone with any knowledge of the jungle around the German bridge it's a ridiculous situation. Our friend Gina has got hold of a simple rustic, as he's traditionally called, and she's doing all she can to cajole him into coming with her to a hotel. The man's tie is hanging loose and he's very drunk. It's a classic situation, and to all the people standing there watching it's clear that the man is about to be expertly ripped off by Gina. An elderly Surinamer, however, with the help of a tall blond man, is trying to put a spanner in the works, and like angry magpies they keep circling around Gina and her prey. Both men are well-known dealers, and this drunk is probably a good client of theirs who buys the girls' favours with cocaine and heroin. They don't want him to be put off coming back. The man remains dopily passive throughout. The confusion reaches a peak when two young policemen pelt up on their racing bikes, misinterpret the situation completely, use their long batons to chase away the dealers and accompany Gina and her victim safely to the place where, as we all know, the real offence will take place in peace and quiet.

Rick and I have heard good things about a new shelter, on the Fokke Simonszstraat. It's only recently opened. When we talk to a few of the people who live there, it seems that the positive reports doing the rounds on the street are no exaggeration. Lou, a resident from day one, speaks highly of the facilities: 'From eight to nine in the morning you get breakfast, but if you don't want to eat you can stay in bed. If you come down at about ten or ten thirty there's coffee, until eleven. You can have a cold lunch from twelve thirty to one thirty, then tea or coffee from two thirty to three, then a hot meal from five thirty to six thirty. Soup, a dessert, meat, veg, potatoes or rice, and if you're still hungry you're allowed seconds. At eight in the evening you get coffee again, until around nine, and later at about ten a cold drink to round off the day.'

We're enthusiastic. This is quite a different matter from the private shelters. It's extraordinarily liberal and residents can come and go as they please. There's just one rule: no drink or drugs inside. Lou has a room of his own, an almost unimaginable luxury. On his bedside table is a snapshot of his children. He's been married twice. 'A wife is nice for a while, but then you have to give her a kick up the arse,' is how Lou looks at it. I ask whether he ever sees his children. He's put all that behind him, he says. He believes they should be the ones to seek contact. 'I certainly think about them all the time, as you can tell by the photo. But if they leave things the way they are, then we'll just have to see who toughs it out longest.'

As we're about to go, Rick is invited to pick a good pair of second-hand shoes.

The next morning Rick has blood on his feet, quite a bit of blood. His new shoes seemed great, but they were definitely too small. He needs another pair, so we decide to try the Bankastraat. The kids from the street, with the help of a church social welfare group, have set up their own centre there, a foundation called Trefpunt ('meeting point'), in the front room of a house belonging to Old Joop and Auntie Riek. The weather is fine, and Old Joop is sitting on the steps along with Barend and a couple of other lads, drinking lager and chocolate milk, while an older Moroccan has his hair cut by one of the boys. 'Buddha', they call him, and he's been tramping the streets here for three years because he's an illegal immigrant. 'I've had a shower, now the haircut. It's great,' says Buddha.

In the living room you can get old clothes, there's coffee, and on Wednesdays a social worker comes round to deal with day-to-day problems. Old Joop used to be homeless himself, so he knows what he's talking about: 'The boys don't like rules. That's just the way it is.' Barend calls out from behind his beer: 'This is all voluntary work; we do it all in our free time.' They've placed their hopes in a chair project. They'll set up a large room with a hundred chairs where you can spend the night in the dry and warm, and get a mug of soup. 'Why not just give everybody a bed?' I ask, but Old Joop thinks that's a ridiculous idea. 'Once you start on beds you need a building the length of the Bankastraat, just for the beds alone. A chair is good too, isn't it? If it's really wet, or freezing cold, then I'm happy enough if I can just sit inside in the warm on a chair.'

Rick takes a shower, his feet are bandaged by Auntie Riek and we even find him another pair of shoes. Meanwhile I get talking with Buddha. 'I haven't got a home or anything,' he says. 'I get coffee and clothes here, everything I'm wearing is from here. We get soup here too and sometimes a blanket.' Occasionally he sleeps with friends for a few weeks, but he always ends up under a bridge again. He doesn't qualify for state benefits, so he can't pay rent. 'Not enough money, lack of money, so okay then, out on the street,' says Buddha. The scissors clip away. 'It's good. Short. Nice weather now. Warm. Short hair.'

The chair project started a few weeks later and quickly closed down again. Every night the room – not much more than a large classroom – was full to bursting with sitting, slumping, half-prone figures, more than a hundred a night and up to twice that if it was cold and wet. The situation quickly proved untenable. Not because someone tore the radiators off the wall in a rage, or smashed all the windows with a chair, roaring and sobbing as he went about it. They were used to that kind of thing. And the complaints from the neighbours and the continual police raids – they could have done something about all that too. The real panic among the people crammed together inside originated on the outside. More and more often, gangs of strong, well-dressed Moroccan boys arrived in the evenings, and in the dark of night they went through the guests' clothes with a sharp knife – addicts sleep particularly deeply – and disappeared with the money and passports.

Before the last of the guests were sent back out onto the street, they were invited to leave a note. 'I've been sleeping outside the railway station for fifteen years. Here I could sleep in the quiet and warm. It's still cold and I'm getting older,' wrote Allal Zagli. Mustapha X declared: 'I think it's bad that you have to close. Everyone will be sleeping on the street again and stealing from the tourists, so the police are sure to have problems.' And an anonymous stroke of the pen read: 'More! Order! Activities!' Toshchin Ohio, a Nigerian car mechanic, described coming to the city at the start of the year to try his luck. After he'd paid his last hotel bill and found himself on the street, he came here. 'I didn't have even a five cent coin left, but they got me through it,' he wrote. 'May Almighty God reward them with eternal life.'

Some guests continued to hang around for weeks, camping in the bushes near the closed shelter, shivering under scraps of plastic sheeting in the rain.

To anyone living on the street, every new day is full of immediate dangers, narrow escapes and near disasters. The plastic bag with those few official papers you possess is suddenly stolen. You run into problems with welfare payments and health insurance. Behind the Central Station, where you'd just found a sleeping place, the police have suddenly started chasing people away again. Your last coin has disappeared, and with it, after a cold night, your last chance of a cup of coffee and a sandwich.

The street is a jungle in which a vagrant can survive only if he or she takes great care or becomes sufficiently streetwise, which the older among them usually are. That was one of the first lessons I learned.

I also learned fairly quickly just how much you can see, even as a complete layman, simply by spending the night dozing on a bench. Every irregularity in the street scene stands right out. Policemen in plain clothes look completely incongruous. If it's not their rather too spick-and-span clothing, then it's their posture that gives them away, burly stance, head up, 'the street belongs to us'. A genuine vagrant always has the street against him.

One day a letter arrived from the social services that suddenly threw Rick's entire income into doubt. For several weeks he'd been staying in a caravan, and after a great deal of hassle he'd managed to get it recognized as an address where he could receive benefit payments. But now a bureaucrat at social services called Scheurvliet had come to check, failed to find Rick's caravan, and decided it had never existed and that 'therefore' Rick had no fixed abode. He'd called Rick in to see him and they'd ended up playing a game of 'yes it does; no it doesn't'. Rick, as the weaker party, inevitably lost, and

Scheurvliet firmly declined the invitation to go along with him and take a look. Rick had 'lied', so his payments would be withheld.

I'd rarely seen Rick as despondent in all those weeks as he was after that conversation. 'What on earth are they up to for god's sake,' he kept wailing. 'You've finally got a roof over your head, even if it's only a caravan, and then they force you to go and sleep in a park or under a bridge again. What is it they want from me?'

Problems come, but they also go, disappearing like soap bubbles. Situations are reviewed and examined by strange commissions and agencies, social workers talk and make phone calls and arrange things, and the problems are forgotten again. Mystifying news does the rounds, every day. We hear that Karel has been picked up because on the fourth of May, Remembrance Day, he got drunk and shouted 'fascists' at the guard of honour. And Henkie Earring was robbed by the Schouten brothers, who lay in wait for him as he collected a holiday payment, part of his disability benefit, from the bank.

Sometimes you run into everyone on the street, at other times no one's about. On the twenty-fifth or the twenty-seventh, for example, those declared unfit for work get paid and everyone goes to the bar. In a world in which everyone haggles all day over single guilders, a tenner at most, a payment of a thousand or fifteen hundred guilders is completely beyond the usual realm of thought. The unevenness of existence is smoothed out in no time. At bars like Rooie Nelis, Emmelot, Corso and Dijk 120, all the boys play at being mayor of Amsterdam, and in May the party is twice as wild, since that's when holiday money falls due. Within about four days, almost everyone is back to the old level of subsistence – ten-cent coins, quarters, and the occasional cadged twenty-five.

The one comfort is that after a few days the fun will start again, when the people on unemployment benefits get their money. But when Rick and I take a walk one payday, there's no one to be found in the bars. We've heard rumours that the whole lot left that morning for the beach at Zandvoort immediately after payment time, to have a nice drink, sitting around a fire in the dunes. The only one we come upon in the street is Hilga from The Hague. Small, half-naked, desperate, sick with withdrawals, not a single client yet today – won't we please lend her a twenty-five? 'Please, please, then I can buy a wrap. I'm starting to crash. You'll get it back on Friday, really. Help me. I'm sick as a dog, love. Just a twenty-five, then I can get a wrap, you really will get it back on Friday, I'm so sick, please.' We succumb. She gives us wet kisses. She's terribly relieved. She tells us a joke in return, a home-made joke. 'This guy comes home, to his lady, and he's brought a bunch of flowers, right? Ah, says his chick; I guess this means I have to spread my legs again. You'd have done better to bring a pig.'

For a short time everything seems to have changed. Thanks to the tireless efforts of a social worker, Rick has bagged a proper place to live, a nice little apartment in East. He's already got the keys in his pocket and he goes around playing with them all day.

'I'm going home soon,' he says, at least six times.

But the next day he turns up looking distraught. Just as he was about to sign the rental contract, it suddenly turned out that he'd have to pay a deposit of 200 guilders. He doesn't have that kind of money because his welfare payments still haven't been sorted, and Scheurvliet refused to help him out, so he's had to hand back the keys to his dream.

Now we're walking again. It's dark and Rick is grousing about the whole world. Some money was stolen from him yesterday, too. Rick's story is not entirely clear this time. Street folk fib and gossip so much that you have to knock quite a bit off the apparent truth value of everything you hear. If in normal situations and with normal people perhaps five or ten per cent of what's said is untrue, on the street the proportion quickly rises to forty per cent, which makes for a fairly peculiar view of the world.

I want coffee, but there's none around at two thirty in the morning, except at prices not intended for the ordinary mortal.

Of the six phone boxes in front of the Central Station, four are occupied this time. Rick bangs bad-temperedly on one of the doors, having made out the face of someone he knows.

We meet a man who is keeping an eye on his girlfriend as she walks the streets. He pays for her upkeep. 'That's fine,' he says. 'But if she wants stuff, then she has to earn it herself, on her back.' If a client picks her up, he's prepared to drive behind them for safety's sake. His goodwill stretches that far.

At the back of the station the cheapest junkie prostitutes are picked up in the most expensive cars. Rick earned a living here for months by writing down the number on the license plate every time a girl got in. If she wasn't back within an hour he was to alert the police. Five guilders a time.

On a metal loading platform, four boys are lying under some plastic, a few bits of cardboard and one sleeping bag. Here and there an arm or a head sticks out of the pile of rags. Rick is finding it hard to come back to this place. He's shaken.

'The shame,' he says. 'The shame you feel.' This is where Rick started his life as a vagrant in 1987. He slept here for almost a year, always with the same group of six men, all but one of them beginners at street life. Of the six, two, Alex and Klaas, have developed over the years into what are known as rubbish bins, shooting up and snorting on top of a solid basis of alcoholism. The third, Old Martin, fled after he'd stolen from practically everybody on the street at least once. He's now sleeping under a bridge somewhere in the east of the country. And two of the six are dead. After two years of frequenting the Pill bridge, Gerrit from Brabant bought enough pills for a month, swallowed them in one go and crept away to the steps of homeless shelter De Regenboog to die. A year later, Marcel died suddenly of cardiac arrest, at thirty-two. At his funeral, somewhere in North Holland, a van arrived with all the lads in it, and the story goes that it was the same kind of show as for Daan, who succumbed to cirrhosis of the liver and had his coffin laid on Heineken crates, with a Heineken flag draped over it. He'd ordered an ocean of half-litre bottles for the bar, for all the guys, as much as they wanted.

On the German bridge someone comes up to us to ask if anyone is willing to go with one of the girls to a hotel room for a bit. Just long enough for her to have a shot. To combat drug use, girls are allowed into the hotels only with clients, so this is a ruse that allows them to make use of a room after they've dealt with the real client and quickly bought a wrap of heroin. The fake punter gets a couple of guilders in return or, if he likes, a free quickie. It means girls will quite often do two tricks for one wrap of heroin and – for those who like to keep track of AIDS statistics – the number of sexual contacts can reach many dozens in a couple of days.

Most of the girls rapidly become hardened once they're on the street. 'You should have seen her three years ago; what a beauty, and a sweet nature too,' I regularly heard experienced street people say as we watched another skinny woman walk past, wobbling on a pair of trodden-down stilettos. The only exception I met in all those weeks was Hilga. With her small, heavy, thickset body she often failed to find a client out there behind the Central Station, but she always kept her spirits up. Everyone laughed at her, but she remained warm and open-hearted. If you lent her money, you could be sure she'd do something for you in return one fine day. When she was at rock bottom, she sometimes let five Turks in a row have their way with her for two twenty-fives, but somewhere inside she retained something that was still unaffected, something the world could never get its claws into.

One evening, after a warm day in May, the weather suddenly turned. A cold wind got up and it started to rain. On the Amstelveld we came upon Meindert, an amiable older man we'd sat chatting with a number of times. Wearing a T-shirt and shorts, he sat shivering on a bench, his legs bare, with six large bottles of lager in front of him. 'Own fault,' he sighed. He'd gone through his benefit money in a few days and used up his four nights at Help for the Homeless for the month as well. 'It's our own fault we're here, all of us.' Old Joop from the Bankastraat had kept him company for a while. Now we'd come to sit with him.

Rick tried to teach Meindert a few crafty ways of finding a bed for the night – 'Get a note from the Maltesers' first aid post. You've enough of a cough,' – but Meindert had given up listening to any advice. 'Give me another beer against the cold, boys, and keep me company for a bit, it's lonely, a whole night like this.'

On the other side of the Amstelveld, Tall Karel appeared, wrapped in a big yellow blanket. He checked out a litter bin, found an old sausage-roll wrapper, licked it and put it back. 'Now, now, now,' all three of us mumbled. 'You can sink pretty low,' Meindert said.

Gradually it grew colder and darker. We bought a few more cans for Meindert and then left him there on his bench. We walked on for a while then turned back, and Meindert was still sitting there, with his bare legs and his T-shirt.

In the living rooms on the far side of the square, the lights came on one by one.

Three afternoons with Henk Plenter

Monday afternoon

I have permission to accompany Henk Plenter on his rounds, Henk Plenter of the public health service. We spend our afternoons driving through the city in his white van, a pile of folders on the front seat, radio-telephone at the ready, criss-crossing the tram rails, since you're allowed to drive on the tramline if you're with the public health department. Sometimes we stop and park the van at a discreet distance from where we're going. We ring the bell and when the front door opens yet another surprise awaits: will it be rotting food this time, old rubbish sacks, a stink of sweat or just a slightly stale smell? When we get back into the van and head for the next address we consider the case between us. 'Cat litter,' I say. 'Overripe litter tray.' 'Nonsense,' says Henk Plenter. 'Mouse pee, pure and simple.' Plenter knows. He's been doing these rounds for twenty-five years. I won't argue.

At the last place there was no room for doubt. Old dog basket. It was definitely old dog basket, we both agreed about that. An elderly man with clear eyes and a polite if ironic tone of voice opened the door, dressed only in his underpants. The windows facing the walkway were murky and indoors the air was brown and acrid. In the front room were piles of books – *Eurocommunism*; a biography of politician Wim Aantjes –

and in the kitchen we found large boxes of rubbish, rotting food, and a sea of cockroaches. In the cupboard were family snapshots, photos of children, a large portrait of a beautiful statuesque woman, seemingly from the 1950s, and on the table a coffee maker covered in cobwebs. The neighbours had complained. The man mumbled something about doing the shopping every week and about a son who was 'working on' helping him clean up. We left. 'Can't do anything. Won't do anything. Hopeless.'

The day before yesterday, a Turkish man in a flat in West, a devout Muslim, was murdered by his son who wanted a Dutch lifestyle. The boy had been arrested and the body removed, but the bed was soaked and the rest of the bloody mess still needed to be cleaned up. The mother was present at the time, on the sofa, petrified, fingering a string of beads. A knife was found under the father's mattress, and not such a small one at that.

Yesterday it was a disturbed girl in South-East: leaks, stench, a sofa soaked in her urine. The psychiatrist on call refused to have her hospitalized because she 'presented no immediate danger to herself or to others'.

Now Plenter is banging on the door of an upstairs apartment on the Overtoom. Boxes are piled up outside, full of old food, empty tin cans and mouse droppings, looking like Don Giovanni's ghost: 'Public health! Plenter here!' Thump, thump, thump. Silence. 'Plenter here!' Silence. We try sniffing through the letter box. It's old dog basket again, but this time a bit sour, mixed with the smell of Voortrekker tobacco. The silence is deafening.

More than half the residents of Amsterdam live on a minimal income, and a quarter of the population of working age is excluded from the world of work. According to the statistics they form the bottom layer of society, but in reality you can distinguish between all kinds of groups and classes, ranging from reasonably satisfied elderly people to aggressive, marginalized young men. So a system has arisen that is taking on more and more of the characteristics of a caste-based society, a world of closed groups each of which can be very hard to escape, where the problem is not so much a lack of material things as a lack of contacts and relationships, of social networks.

The very bottom layer consists of an extremely diverse collection of runaway youngsters, newcomers, vagrants, addicts and the seriously psychologically disturbed. They all have one thing in common; for one reason or another they have such inadequate social networks that there's nobody who cares. How many people are in that situation and what exactly goes on in such groups no one knows. They are the dregs, the pariahs of a society that is increasingly split into separate strata.

Anyone descending into this underworld with Henk Plenter needs to keep both eyes wide open, and very often their nose held tight shut.

Every week some ten reports come in and every day Plenter drives out to investigate. 'Complaints in West. Hmm,' he mumbles as we're manoeuvring through the traffic on the Weteringschans. 'A collector in a houseboat. We've already evicted him once. A moth plague in South. Stench and cockroaches in the Kinker neighbourhood – I know that one. Nasty old guy. Causes the neighbours no end of trouble. We'll have to go and see.'

Plenter is a cheerful man, approaching fifty, the robust type every branch of officialdom relies on for work in the field. His department is where all complaints about neighbours end up, from all over the city – those that concern dirt, infestation or smell, at least. His clients often don't want to be helped, or can't be helped because everything has already been done. With gentle pressure, and the threat of eviction as the ultimate big stick, he often manages to get somewhere. Sometimes a cleaning company is called in, sometimes arrangements are made with a psychiatrist or a community police officer, but even the options open to a welfare state have their limits.

'Public health department! Plenter here!' Through the letter box we eventually hear coughing. 'I'm not opening the door. I'm not opening the door. Who is it?' 'Public health.' 'You're not coming in!' 'Mr Pieterse, I only wanted to have a talk with you.' 'Just bugger off!'

Henk Plenter has a remarkable gift:, no one ever asks him for identification. Sailing in and out of this world of filth and loneliness, he's a true professional – you can tell at a glance. He's calm and pleasant, 'but if the need arises I can be mean as hell'.

Within a minute we're inside, face to face with a doddery old man. His brown dressing gown is half open, his face covered in blotches and eczema. The apartment is almost pitch dark and stifling hot; every possible space is stuffed full of old clothes, rags and papers, and on top of it all is a greasy layer of total neglect with which I'll soon become extremely familiar. The man is at a loss. He trembles and snorts like a sick old cat. 'Just you bugger off!' 'I'm leaving shortly.' 'Out, damn you, filthy bastards!' 'Less of the anger, man.' 'Drop dead!'

There turns out to be a relative in the flat, and mental health services will try to make some kind of arrangement with him. They'll have to be quick. The rags and papers are right next to the gas heater; the whole lot could go up in flames any minute. 'Now get out, you shits. Drop dead!'

'He's still wearing the same clothes as four years ago,' says Plenter when we get outside.

This is turning into a regular dirty-old-man afternoon.

In West we come upon a man of about thirty, dressed in black plastic trousers, a T-shirt, and a green knitted cardigan held shut by a belt. *The Oprah Winfrey Show* is on. The man sucks irascibly at his pipe. 'I've got two dogs and no one else to help me. Good thing too. I don't want anyone and I don't need anyone.'

A rancid smell of diarrhoea pervades the house. There are two dogs, two rabbits, two turtles, a pair of pigeons and five cats. We walk into the yard outside, to the rabbit hutches. 'You'll leave those animals alone!' 'That remains to be seen.' 'Watch it. If you touch them, there's going to be some kind of accident.' 'Wipe that door down with bleach. Do something, man!' says Plenter. 'I only have time at weekends.'

The walls inside are covered in paintings: a meadow; Jesus at the last supper; Elvis Presley. There's a cupboard full of ornaments and Matchbox toys, and everything is covered in dust. On a side table are porn magazines, great piles of them.

Earlier in the afternoon, along with Plenter's boss, we looked at photographs from the department's files. Collectors are people who pick things up off the street and take them home until the place is completely full and almost everything is buried and inaccessible.

'This was an old man who thought he had a duty to put food out for all the animals, including rats and mice.' Six pairs of cat eyes stared out roguishly from a pile of boxes, looking straight at the camera. 'This one was truly filthy. An alcoholic. The house was literally dripping with old vomit.'

'No one knows how many such people there are in the city,' the boss said. 'We get the addresses only if they cause a nuisance, otherwise you never hear about them.' Every year they deal with about two hundred serious cases. 'But the number of fully justified complaints is definitely increasing,' said Henk Plenter.

The boss talked about people they find crawling on the floor who can no longer do anything for themselves, yet don't want to be helped. 'There's no compulsory care in this country. That's a good principle to have, but we see the other side,' she said. Henk Plenter added: 'And what about people who rage against society, refuse psychiatric help and pour buckets of muck out of the windows? There are people we've evicted five times, people who can't be put into psychiatric institutions but are nevertheless a huge pain in the arse. They refuse all forms of assistance. That's our main problem.'

More photos: an apartment in East, rats everywhere, the chewed corpses of two pit-bulls and a cat; a photo of a desiccated dead cat, left in a shower by people who moved out, the legs splayed, the mouth open in a scream.

We drive along the tracks of Tram 3 to the Indische neighbourhood. With his free hand Henk Plenter rearranges the files on the front seat. The next report concerns the opposite of a collector, a woman who, screaming and swearing, keeps throwing everything in her apartment out of the window.

When we arrive a whole delegation has gathered at her door, a social worker, someone from the housing association and another man from the public health department.

We go upstairs and find that the psychiatrist has already talked to her. She's taken a pill. She has calmed down. She's very grateful, she says now. The place is freezing cold. There's no heating. Nor are there any tables or chairs, no pots and pans, not a knife nor a fork. There's nothing at all in the flat. On the plywood floor lie a mattress and a blanket, and on the counter is a small camping-gas bottle. That's all. The trees front and back are hung with clothes, rags, scraps of plastic, underwear, bits of sanitary towel and toilet paper, all waving in the wind like bizarre Christmas decorations.

'Complaints from South about moths,' it says on the next form. We turn into a neat, quiet street near the Hilton Hotel. The neighbours have been complaining. The top floor is rented out and the rent is always paid on time, but no one can remember ever seeing the tenant. Four years ago a new lock was put on the street door, but she never came to fetch the key.

Last week painters were at work in the building. They opened a door and it was only then that the neighbours downstairs understood where all those moths were coming from.

We go up. When we step inside it's as if time has stood still and the air along with it. It's dry as a desert. So this is what a nice apartment in Old South looks like when, for some unaccountable reason, life is suddenly sucked out of it and no one sets foot in the place for more than six years. Everything, every single thing, is covered in a thin layer of dust: books, furniture, bedclothes, a copy of *De Telegraaf* dated 9 May 1985, a half-eaten hand towel, a small table with jewellery and perfume bottles, toothbrushes, soap, cotton wool, all neat and tidy, and everything covered with that thin, white film of dust and the stagnant air of 9 May 1985.

Wednesday afternoon

A report came in from the Salvation Army a day or so ago. In Old West a man was supposed to have his power cut off, but the electrician refused to work in the place because of the stench. Henk Plenter went to look and someone from social services opened the door. He'd only just gone inside – the man had hanged himself. The body was already 'leaking' as the jargon has it. 'Around sixty, I'd say. The house wasn't even particularly dirty. Bit of a bachelor pad, pretty austere, really. He did it with a length of electrical cable.'

Lonely deaths are quite common in Amsterdam. Anyone who accompanies Plenter for a while will come upon one. Some forty times a year his department's staff will come across a body. On a sofa in a living room in East, Plenter recently found an old client of his. The man had moved house and at that point Plenter lost track of him. He was completely mummified. He'd been lying there for a year and a half. In a district of new houses Plenter found an elderly man who turned out to have been sitting next to the body of his dead brother for six weeks. They'd lived together all their lives, more or less as hermits. The other brother has since died too. In a student house Plenter found the body of a girl who must have been dead for at least ten months.

In winter especially, that kind of thing can go unnoticed. 'Most of them dry out quite quickly, especially if there's a heater turned on, with the inevitable results. Sometimes you have to work in an overall and boots, sometimes bits of bed or carpet have to be cut away along with the body.'

But this afternoon we have to move on. There's been a complaint about a collector in a houseboat, an old client. We find him in a chair outside, a man with a grey beard and a blue smock, a Russian army hat on his head, his right pocket stuffed full of diaries and official papers. Pigeons and seagulls patter at his feet. His home is filled to the ceiling with furniture, newspapers, plastic rubbish sacks, cloths and rags, bedclothes, polystyrene foam, old books and birdcages. The roof is scattered with old garden chairs, scrap wood, shopping trolleys and ancient television sets.

'I'm from a Jordanian family of fascists,' he says. 'That's right, that guy De Vries of the security services, he's my brother. It's true. We came out of the same telescope.' He usually sleeps outside, he tells us, or on the roof. 'But these days I get quite a bit of trouble from those bleepers, those little telephones, the ones you can't hear, only the police can.'

Plenter warns him something has to be done, otherwise he'll be evicted again, but the conversation soon turns to homosexuality in the army and the police, which seems to worry the man in the Russian hat a good deal. He expounds upon his theories for us, at a cracking pace. 'You've got those faggot groups, who get you to go with a beautiful girl, except that then you have to screw them as well, from behind. The whole police force is full of them.'

On cold nights he sleeps indoors. 'How do you get in?' we ask. He twists at his nose with his fingers: 'Jiggle-joggle, follow your nozzle.' He removes a tarpaulin, somewhere near a window. 'They're in the army too. They all end up with ulcers on their arses. But you can count me out, I'm sixty-five and I don't go along with it any more, which is why they're after me.'

Beyond the tarpaulin, in a tightly packed mass of newspapers and rags, a small round opening is revealed, a worn cavity just big enough for someone to lie in, curled up, a man-sized mouse hole.

We drive on again in the white van to see about a complaint in Betondorp. Henk Plenter is in an optimistic mood. Last week he discovered an elderly man in New West that he's sure he can do something about. 'I'm certain. We'll hire a cleaning company, get a doctor, it'll all work out fine.' There had been quite a stench, the man opened the door naked, everything was sticky, his nails were long, his feet were a dreadful sight, 'and he was immensely rich, really a lovely man'. 'Why do you live like this?' Plenter tried. 'With your kind of money you could go and lie on a beach in the Bahamas with a tasty lady.' But the man said that wasn't the way he was.

It turned out that his friend had died ten years earlier and since then he'd been going out only twice a week, to shop. He no longer dared to pick up the phone. 'More than once I've seen people like that have all their money taken by a couple of young kids,' says Plenter, swerving onto the tram tracks with an adroit turn of the wheel. 'This one's fortunate to be so shy. But I'll help him to get on top of it all, without too much trouble. I'm sure of it.'

We bounce over the bridge across the Amstel and drive past a boarded-up house on the Weteringschans. 'That's where the

Chosen of the People of Israel used to live,' Henk Plenter tells me. He'd been inside the house. She had something against the Surinamese family that lived downstairs. They were of Satan and she tried to drive them away with Lysol, which was where he came in.

'I got along fine with her. She thought I was a little like Christ, she said. She'd made a kind of temple in the living room, with tapestries and beautiful old icons, and an altar with candles and above it an arch with Christ on the cross.' He visited her about five times, and the place certainly wasn't dirty, it was just that she had to stop using that Lysol. 'So I said to her, "But how would you like it if your whole house smelled of Lysol all the time?" And she said to me, "But how would you like it if you found big green puddles of devil's snot outside your door every morning?" '

In Betondorp we drink tea with a retired Dutch Labour Party couple, sitting cosily by the gas fire. The clock ticks. He tells us about a children's playground association in which he still plays an active part and she talks about the neighbourhood they helped to build up, and about the trouble they now have with the people upstairs who keep tipping their urine out of the window. It makes yellow streaks on the outside of their window panes.

Thirty centimetres above this peaceful scene, we come upon a brother and sister, somewhere in an indefinable phase of life between forty and seventy. It's baking hot, the mynah bird is screeching while a commercial television station broadcasts a Brazilian soap about a surrogate mother. The brother sits silently at the window, thin, with long, grey, straggly hair. The sister, dressed in pyjamas that have fallen open around her belly, has her nose glued to the screen, beer within reach.

Plenter says he's going to take action if they don't stop that business with the piss. The woman denies it. 'We've got two beautiful children, the two of us, and I swear on their lives that I'm telling the truth.' Plenter stands his ground. The woman replies, 'Hope you get cancer. I want you to die, you bastard.' Plenter shouts, the woman shouts, the mynah bird shouts, while the man on the sofa shakes his head back and forth. 'Wooo,' he says. 'Wooo.'

A few streets away we have another collector, but this time he's a so-called 'organizing collector'. He's not at home, but his world lives and breathes. Through the living-room window we can see that the floor is covered in clocks and timers, lined up like a pink and pale-blue army. The hundreds of second hands have a weird regularity to them. On the wall of the shed a cuckoo clock is ticking; the garden table presents a still life of two keys, several wristwatches and an alarm clock; in the garden are bicycles, upside down, their wheels turning in the wind, and beneath them more alarm clocks and watches, partially buried in the ground, alive, dead or half-dead.

'I forgot to finish telling you the story about the Chosen on the Weteringschans,' says Henk Plenter when we're sitting in his van again.

One day he had to go back because she'd erected all kinds of signs on her balcony and the whole lot was so unstable that it threatened to fall at any moment. 'Weteringschans, no brothel,' one sign said. Another: 'Satan, leave me.' From time to time she would stand on the balcony, shouting: 'God's wrath. God's wrath will strike you down. I am the vengeance of the Lord.'

She was very angry when, accompanied by a policeman who also knew her well, Plenter came to remove the signs. In the end she capitulated. 'I'll let you remove them, but the wrath of the Lord will strike you down.'

That night she stood out there again, shouting. Then at four in the morning, when the city was utterly silent, the house was suddenly transformed into a hellish inferno. The policeman who knew her happened to be on duty and he saw her standing there, on the balcony, arms spread wide. 'Jump, jump,' he shouted, but she turned around. She picked up her dog and held it in her arms. The last anyone saw of her was a shadow against the flames.

Friday afternoon

Several months later, and the smell has finally gone from my hands.

Meanwhile much has happened. The tenant of the forgotten white-dusted apartment in South was located after a bit of searching and she's now started to clean it up. The man on the houseboat has received a summons to say he must clear his rubbish away within a month. The ironic elderly man in the flat has straightened things out a bit with the help of his son, and the woman in the Indische neighbourhood who threw everything out of the windows now has regular counselling, of her own free will. But the angry man near the Overtoom is not doing well at all, and no one can get into his house any longer.

Lonely deaths continue to present themselves: a junkie in a foldaway bed in the Jordaan, a solitary old man with a colostomy bag, and elsewhere in the city there was an antiques dealer in a house full of cobwebs who must have been winding up an old pendulum clock when it fell on his head. His dog was nearby, also dead. They'd lain there for weeks, all those dead bodies, and the same fate befell an elderly homosexual in New West. 'I found him myself, naked, in the kitchen,' Henk Plenter says. 'We'd done all we could. It was inevitable, you could tell. The man didn't want to go on.' It's almost always men who end up that way, not women, he tells me. 'Strange, huh?'

There's been trouble with a couple of collectors. We'd visited one of them before, in Bos and Lommer. The boxes, rags and old newspapers were piled up in the four rooms to about half a metre from the ceiling, and the woman who opened the door complained that she couldn't go into town any longer because her bicycle had got buried somewhere in one of the rooms, under the boxes. She's now sorted things out somewhat. But two other collectors, a man and his girlfriend in East, both aged around eighty, had serious plans to kill Plenter. 'You said you were going to do it,' Plenter heard one of them whisper to the other. 'No, you did. You promised.' 'Are you talking about me?' Plenter asked. 'Yes, you,' they replied. 'You ought to be killed. You're a bad man.'

There had once been an old woman who was always throwing things out of the windows and arguing with her neighbour, talking angrily to him as if he wasn't there, as if he was a ghost only she could see.

There were twin sisters in the Jordaan, both well over seventy, who were firmly convinced their mother was still alive. 'She's just gone to do some shopping at Albert Heijn.' 'Yes, if anyone rings and mother's there, tell her we've gone to the Westerstraat.' 'So is your father still alive too?' 'Yes, he is, but we don't let him in any longer.' According to the marriage license floating around in the flat, their father would have been a hundred and five.

We set off again. There's a report from the Wallen. A television technician has found an elderly woman in an upstairs flat who can't cope any more. The pimp downstairs swears, amid the nipple clamps and bottles of Spanish fly, that there's nothing wrong with her. 'But there is such a thing as looking out for each other a bit,' says Henk Plenter.

In South a woman is having difficulty with her neighbours' enormous mess. But apart from a box with a few old newspapers on the shared staircase, there's nothing to be seen. The woman who rang the department is in her early forties and her complaint is about the family upstairs, 'Girls of eighteen or twenty who wander the streets and come home at four or six in the morning'. We listen patiently as the stories gush over us: doctor's notes, rental contracts and decisions about welfare payments. 'I used to go out sometimes, with my brother, but then you'd be in a group of young people and you'd know all of them.'

The room is small. The cane chairs are draped with white covers, the tablecloth is yellow and pink. 'We used to have a housewife living upstairs but she couldn't cope with it either. Eventually they put her in hospital.' In the cupboard are three dictionaries, on the coffee table a pink ashtray with a red lighter inscribed 'Test the West'. A ticking clock. Outside I can hear the distant sound of a tram.

We drive out to the edge of the city. Between a motorway, an old village church and the railway stands a wooden shed surrounded by discarded timber, tyres, wheels, gas bottles, scrap metal, here and there a window box, a broomstick with a doll's head on it, and at least ten cats wandering about amidst it all. Engines emit smoke. There are fires of scrap wood and old tyres.

An old man comes towards us. They've been living here since the 1950s, he and his wife. Their children grew up here, but now his wife has been in bed for six months and he can hardly do anything because of his back.

Last week they had tons of rubbish removed. They never hear from their children these days. 'She's in a bad way,' he whispers. 'Since Friday she's done nothing but vomit.'

Inside it's almost dark. There's a piercing stench of urine. Outside the diggers in the Slotervaart district grind and rumble. In the corner lies an elderly woman on a pile of rags, half-covered by a blanket. To judge by her voice she's from Aerdenhout, the wealthiest town in the Netherlands. 'Are you a doctor, sir? Who sent you, the police? It's a terrible mess here, I know, but please don't be angry right now.'

Henk Plenter softly tries to reassure her and mutters that something has to happen here urgently, no later than tomorrow. 'How about we just put you in bed for a week, in hospital, to let them have a good look at you, give you a nice wash.'

In the shack the remains of a convivial past are in evidence everywhere, a television, an open hearth with a mantelpiece, a radio, cheerful postcards. But everything is covered in a thick layer of grease and the floor is muddy and slippery with excrement.

'I was born in 1920,' she says. 'What is it now, 1990? Oh, 1992 already? Then I must be seventy-two. Please excuse me. I'm a bit naughty in my head.'

One thing stands out amid the chaos – there are flowers everywhere. In among the hairy blankets, the cats, the flies and the slippery floor, plants are flowering, miniature roses, azaleas, daffodils, chrysanthemums. Everywhere too are the oranges and bananas the man, in his desperation, has been stocking up on with great persistence, none of them touched.

Henk Plenter cautiously tries to raise the woman's heavy body a bit, improvising a pillow out of a bundle of rags and the least dirty blanket. He promises to send help quickly and brushes the flies from her legs.

'That white stuff she brings up. What do you think it is? Would it be bile?' the man whispers.

The woman sits up a little in bed. 'My God,' she moans. 'Glorious God, glorious God, glorious God.' And then, 'You aren't angry, are you sir? Please don't be angry, please sir, please, please. Don't be angry, not angry.'

The island

You can walk across the island in five minutes and even the length of it takes less than half an hour. It's connected to the rest of the world by a bridge and a narrow causeway. At the town hall, far away in the city centre, it exists only as a world of drawings and scale-models, populated by a new, brilliant and beautiful species of human being. But that's not the world we're talking about now.

At the time when these events took place, the monarchs of the isle were still called Aidy, Patrick, Jan, Karel, Carly, Franklin, Josephine and the Cakebaker. Their palaces were of great beauty. Their deeds were spirited and wild and are spoken of to this day, in the remotest corners of Europe: in lonely tents in Leefland, in the cold, abandoned factories of Kreuzberg, on Portugal's quietest beaches and beside the fires that burn every night in the wasteland beyond the Teleport office development.

Anyone wanting to get to the island has to take the exit on the wrong side of the Central Station, the side where Henny sometimes street-walks if she's not too out of it. Keep on along the waterfront, past the empty warehouses where the scent of coconut, cocoa and far distant lands still lingers, past a fortress-like building with tall railings, once built as a hotel for destitute Russian emigrants waiting for the ship to take them to a new life, past a row of houses with little gardens that smell of forsythia and soap powder, past an abandoned marshalling yard where an old Belgian goods wagon is still rusting away between the thistles, the wind always blowing as if it's Nova Zembla and finally, after walking all that way, you come to a place to which only a few initiates have the key.

Here lies the battlefront of manual labour, such as every city has, desolate and forgotten, a place between leaving and being trapped, a district that bears traces of the work of thousands of human lives yet there's not a mortal soul to be seen.

For anyone wanting to go any further there's only one direction to take: to the other side. To the trees and grass in the distance. To the old warehouses lit up reddish orange by the evening sun.

The island. The buildings are from a period when the terrain – like three quarters of Holland – was reclaimed from the brackish waters of the Zuider Zee by hundreds of sweating, swearing, gin-drinking polder workers from Westphalia and Oldenburg. That was in the late nineteenth century, when the world took possession of the city again and the old harbour burst at the seams.

In 1902 the island became the headquarters of the Royal Dutch Steamboat Company, the KNSM, and so it remained until the mid-1970s, a maze of warehouses, cranes, sacks, crates, ships and trains with at its centre, the company's pride and joy, the canteen, built on tall pillars so that you could easily drive underneath with a load of freight. It had big glass walls looking out over the water, broad steps leading to a room where some fifteen hundred workers and officials could sit down to eat, and a stage large enough to celebrate ten simultaneous silver jubilees.

Another sight worth seeing was the Kompaszaal, the Compass Hall. Until the early 1960s, first-class passengers bound for America or the Dutch East Indies sat there waiting to board. When squatters pulled the planks away from the boarded-up building many years later, the first shafts of light fell on an almost pristine space. The rubber floors, the curves of the bar, the metal tulip lamps, the balcony rails with windlasses for the gangway, the customs hall with scratch marks from cabin trunks still on the floor, the toilets – everything looked the way it would if the doors had been locked after the good ship Oranje sailed off across the IJ on 6 September 1958 or thereabouts and stayed that way until broken open again on a spring day in 1980, by a handful of youngsters from the Transvaal district.

The Open Harbour Museum, the new residents renamed this miraculously preserved relic of the 1950s. They held parties and exhibitions there and showed videos depicting the stories their grandparents told about the island's prehistory. How they worked daily shifts of fourteen or fifteen hours for nine guilders a week, hooked up bales weighing a hundred kilos or more, suffered strange red burns on their shoulders when they carried heavy railway sleepers, soothed the pain with balsam of Peru, breakfasted on 'road-mender' every morning, a whole loaf cut in four with a smear of lard on it. 'God had created rich and poor. We were clearly second-rate. We lived in grinding poverty. My father drummed into us, "Make sure you do your work well. Then you'll be able to go on opening your mouth." '

Other than that it was deathly silent on the island for years, apart from the singing of a few late birds. An occasional ship sailed past on the IJ. On the Devil's Bend at the tip of the island, you might sometimes find a lonely angler. At the dockside, bits of old cardboard blew across the overgrown rails.

At first only a few people knew this world existed. Some of the buildings had once been inhabited in a distant past, but those early settlers didn't know what to do with the huge warehouse spaces and left again, in search of a better place.

Not until the early 1980s did something like permanent occupation begin. Artists built studios in partitioned-off sections of the old canteen which turned out to be ideal workspaces, light, high, with a broad view out over the island and the water beyond. Edelweiss, they called the building.

It was quiet for seven long years. Then a handful of caravans were towed onto the island. They stopped at the best place, under the trees, near the causeway, a little oasis amid the concrete and rust. The caravans were large and well maintained. The new residents quickly started laying out little gardens and most spent their days working or studying in town.

In the spring of the following year the Brits arrived. Solidly encased in leather, they drank beer and proudly displayed their tattoos: arrows, skulls, crosses, or black barbed-wire around the neck. They came from Bradford, a drab city where almost half the men were out of work and it was war every Saturday afternoon on the football terraces. Aidy, Patrick and Maff wanted more on the island than just beer, peace and shelter from the rain. Their home was to become a music venue, and a meeting place for all the outcasts of the earth.

They realized well enough that a certain amount of activity and organization would be required. They welded together two old buses and started to sell pizza – and beer. Then, no one quite knows how, word started to get about.

That spring was a time of burgeoning life. More campers and caravans turned up every day. New arrivals began putting up tents, or moving into huts made of plastic and discarded wood. Large tables appeared outside the bar, which started serving meals – with beer, and beer, and yet more beer. Before very long everyone for miles around was walking about with a half-litre bottle of Leeuw from morning to night, hooked up like a drip.

That bottle of lager was their balsam of Peru. Aidy, Maff, Patrick and some of the other inhabitants of the bar were never seen without one. From an early age they'd become adept at carrying out all kinds of tasks with one hand, including the hauling around of old caravans, the tugging straight of tarpaulins, the sorting of found timber and the removal of unwanted visitors. But what they achieved in those first few weeks was unprecedented. In a Big Bang of one-handed activity they managed to extend the bar using scrap-metal, cast-off timber and plastic sheeting and to turn it into a power centre from which they ruled the island, The Last Bus Shelter, better known as the Busbar.

It was a time of great promise. First the Busbar was given an awning, then another extension. They even added an upper floor, 'the office', with steps up to it and a balcony with a proper convex balustrade all around, fished out of a demolition site somewhere. They built a brick fireplace and then carried a bar inside, even a billiard table.

So in just a few months the Busbar grew into a kind of Palace Flophouse, and the same was true of many other structures. A short distance away a stunning wigwam appeared, made of shiny wood. A guy called Willem built an even more attractive house, with sophisticated variations in floor levels and small windows in the roof, different coloured timbers that formed a mosaic, and a shelf for books. Most of the island's inhabitants lived rather more simply. A leaky tent, a worn-out caravan, a hole in the ground, a sheet of plastic, a few old planks, and a life of freedom and adventure could begin.

Carly, along with Josephine, was one of the original residents. She'd led her own life in her studio in Edelweiss for years. She painted, made art objects and founded and designed a magazine before letting it become defunct. While doing all that she gazed out over the island.

For years there had been nothing but peace and emptiness and sometimes, as she sat at her little coal stove on stormy November nights, the sound of the wind through the ancient cranes. Until that spring arrived.

Carly had always thought she belonged to just about the lowest rank of society, but now an entirely new, super-underclass was gathering beneath her floor. People moved in below the canteen that, as we have seen, the KNSM in its infinite wisdom had built on tall pillars. There were junkies, a heroin-whore who played guitar and a few seriously disturbed alcoholics. The girl soon left again as she was grabbed by all the men every night. The others stayed.

The influx was unrelenting and villages began to form in this new world. When Carly looked out from her studio, she could see directly in front of her, at the water's edge, a hippie-style colony where fires burned and children played. An old barrel served as a shared bath. She named it Tripper Village, to distinguish it from the group that lived directly under her studio, which the islanders simply referred to as The Junkies.

Then there was the German Triangle, a quiet group remarkable only for its powerful territorialism and its liberal purchasing policy. You didn't see much of the boys and the girls seemed to earn good money by doing something unsavoury in a Utrecht sex club. Further along was Pixie Village, a colony of alternatively dressed people who had made little gardens with fences around them and even set up a complete living room in the open air, sofas, armchairs, television sets, all of it bleached by the sun and soaked by the rain.

At the other end, near the entrance to the terrain, were the Founding Fathers, the group with the well-kept caravans, the old elite of Van Buurens and Vanderbilts, who barely associated with anyone else. Occasionally guests were accommodated there – a large British circus family for instance, stranded on its way to Greece when one of the lorries broke down. Husband, wife, children, fools, clowns, acrobats, tricks, rides, rehearsals – it was a robbers' symphony for the island to marvel at every day.

Meanwhile the Busbar had become famous as far away as the beaches of Portugal and Crete. But between the bar and the local squatters – who according to the islanders' sense of history had lived there since time immemorial – relations quickly soured. Bicycles were stolen, windows broken, and of the forty chickens in the collective Edelweiss chicken run, most were soon missing. The Edelweiss building itself was never broken into. That code at least was respected.

Very occasionally, Carly visited the neighbours. James, for instance, who was black and lived beneath her, had constructed a kind of couch in his hut. You could go and sit on it to enjoy a cup of tea and a biscuit, and a good chat. There was a second bar too, right next door, the Busstop, which didn't sell drink, only apple juice and pancakes. The Trippers often visited, and occasionally the people from Edelweiss as well. But usually they stayed upstairs, where they watched night come down slowly over the island, until it was pitch dark and all they could see were dozens of fires and a few vague shadows. You had to rely on the sounds, the eternal comings and goings, the barking of dogs and sometimes, deep in the night, a scream. It had stopped bothering Carly a long time ago, except when real trouble started. Then, as if alerted by a seventh sense, she would wake up, instantly wide awake.

One morning an unknown child was seen wandering around the island, a robust little boy, about seven years old. The next day he was there again. He played outside alone for days, cadging a bit of food here and there before lying down to sleep again in the sun. One evening some people saw him crawl into an abandoned hut, after parking a plastic toy truck neatly in front of the door. There were other children, and some of the mothers started to take care of the little boy to some extent, but some days no one knew where he'd got to. The word on the island was that his parents were addicts and serving time in jail. On a couple of occasions an expensive car was spotted on the terrain at the crack of dawn, with an unknown man at the wheel. The little boy got out and the car drove off. After two months he disappeared as suddenly as he had come.

In the years when all that the city worried about was new catering outlets and the kinds of clothing and conversation that were appropriate in them, I heard of a man who had chosen to renounce the world. He'd withdrawn to a den made of a few planks, behind the zoo. Several rats lived next door, but he didn't regard them as a problem. He kept them on friendly terms – at least, so he thought – by voluntarily donating some of his food: bread, cheese and brown beans. 'It's their place too,' he would say. All went well for several weeks. Then his neighbours started to come on rather strong. One night – he'd been away for the weekend – there was a sudden rustle and a cracking sound, followed by a flood of brown bodies. At least thirty rats, led by a giant female, ran onto and around his bed. All he could do was flee, head over heels. Yet again he had lost his home to superior forces.

On the island, relations between humans and animals were excellent. The rats were friendliness personified. Karel, an old one-legged man with a white goatee who had arrived on a bus from Bodegraven, used a colony of rats that he kept in his mobile home as a foil for his moods. But that was simply for companionship, a way of driving out loneliness ten, twenty, forty, eighty, a hundred and sixty times over.

Dogs were a different matter. Everyone had a dog, preferably two, and the bigger the better. During even the island's quietest hours, between six and nine in the morning, the air was filled with their barking, interspersed with whining and howling when yet another dogfight broke out.

Even Marloes, who lived in a borrowed minibus with her three children, had a bouvier bitch that soon gave birth to two pups, Basje and Thijsje. She adopted an energetic approach to the problem of having two additional mouths to feed. At four o'clock she would take her three children for a free meal at Mother Theresa; then at six they called in at Hare Krishna, and whatever was left she slipped under the table for the dogs.

Many islanders lived in one way or another from the

crumbs that fell from the city, walking from one soup kitchen to the next. They salvaged, sometimes pilfered, ransacked the markets, and burned old electrical cables to sell the copper as scrap. The penetrating smell of burnt plastic hung permanently over the terrain.

Gradually however, the island developed an economy of its own. As the Big Party season approached, with plans fermenting everywhere, there was a flourishing trade in second-hand clothes, sandwiches and lemonade. In a shack under Edelweiss, Bicycle Repair Man moved in, providing an essential service. The real top dog of the hut complex, though, was the Cakebaker, a thickset German, bald with a white jumper, who sure enough had once been a pastry-cook somewhere in Germany but left, or so it was said around the nocturnal fires, 'because he put too much dope in the pastry'. At first he dabbled in pills, but soon he took firm charge and began to bring order to the chaos that had developed within a few months beneath Edelweiss. He saw to it, for example, that bicycles were parked beside bicycles, timber next to timber, bricks adjacent to bricks. At the end of an afternoon of sorting like that, everyone felt extraordinarily content.

The Cakebaker even had an employee, a skinny Englishman who didn't say much and sometimes went off his head after a few tablets. '*Mein Geschäft ist da!*' the Cakebaker used to say proudly to visitors: 'My shop's over there!' And he would point to his hut, which had a few planks in front to support a plastic awning. You could indeed get anything there, from sterile gauze ('borrowed' for 'emergencies' from the first-aid post) to fresh bread bought early at the Dirk van den Broek supermarket for one guilder seventy-nine and sold on the island for two fifty.

In a caravan in front of Edelweiss lived a boy and a girl whose names no one could recall. Both were skin and bone, although she must once have been very pretty. They tried to grow vegetables in a home-made greenhouse. They never removed their rubbish but simply threw everything out of the window, food scraps, old clothes, bicycle parts, hair clasps and medicine bottles. Nearby was an old bathtub they'd got hold of somewhere, and occasionally they filled it with water and lit a fire underneath so that she could enjoy a perfect lukewarm bath. As dinnertime approached you could sometimes see the boy hunting through the rubbish mountain near their caravan. He might straighten up looking pleased, holding an almost empty, yet suddenly absolutely essential, tube of mayonnaise.

The social divide was visible on the island in an almost classical sense. Whoever had electricity had power. Whoever sat in the dark had none. Electricity was scarce, expensive and therefore a much sought after status symbol. The Busbar had electricity, as did the original squatters and a few extremely privileged caravan dwellers. But apart from that, everyone was off the grid. There were no streetlights and none were to be installed, since they would have made the place too attractive. After sunset the average island resident had to make do with a fire, a torch or the odd gas lamp.

The local council didn't need to do anything. The terrain officially belonged to the council's own property development company, the Gemeentelijk Grondbedrijf, but since the government's left hand often prefers not to know what its right hand is doing, all the other council departments – aside from the public health service – declared that the terrain was private property, not a public right of way, and that the private owner (in this case the local council) would have to sort things out for itself.

So the island quickly became an example of what the official jargon of the time called 'government by tolerance'. The police were ordered to intervene as little as possible, so as to avoid 'causing matters to escalate'. The sanitation department had 'neither the intention nor the manpower' to take the island in hand. So state authority was initially limited to a handful of officials who rode around in their council vans, eyes on stalks. Only when the first journalists turned up at the Busbar, and a few city councillors started to stir, did the time become ripe for a gesture.

A year after the Busbar opened a decision was made at the town hall to appoint four council stewards: Aalders and Van den Berg, plus two other gentlemen who won't take any further part in this story, since they were not spotted once on the island after taking up their posts.

We needn't spend too much time on Van den Berg either. He did his job, and far more besides. He was a warm, rotund, calm, practical man of few pretensions, the kind that has kept the city running for centuries. He followed up quickly when trouble arose, made sure there were mobile toilets and a first-aid post, and if there were any real problems he was on the spot immediately. It was he who managed to get the sanitation department to carry out a major cleanup operation on the island after a few months. He did his best to deliver a council missive to that effect (addressed 'to the residents and/or occupiers of the KNSM island') to the caravans, tents and huts, under a door, half-inside a tent, beneath bricks in front of huts and holes in the ground. 'All residents and occupiers are requested to present their refuse wrapped or tied together if at all possible.'

His colleague Aalders, better known as Franklin, assisted him in all this, but he acquired his authority largely by other means. He was one of the residents of the studios, and before the council appointed him to his new post he had achieved a degree of fame within an intimate circle for his Bison glue project in which, coated with paste, he had himself stuck to a wall as an art object.

Franklin lived on the island even before the coming of the Busbar, and he was soon able to buy his way into that particular power base by supplying all the energy the bar needed via a branch line from his electricity meter. It gave him an influential finger in the pie, and by installing him as a steward the local council was making good use of that fact.

Most of the other squatters had a less benevolent attitude. It was after all their electricity that breathed life into the Busbar's amplifiers, ghetto-blasters and equalizers. Not everyone had the same enthusiasm for the bar's ability to carry on playing 'The All Out Nuclear Holocaust Show', 'Fury in the Slaughterhouse' or 'Esmeralda's Edible Underwear' into the early hours. Some of the squatters even demanded absolute silence on the island after ten thirty – which was odd, given that most of them had until recently been eager participants in the far from sedate nightlife of the city centre.

Franklin had an approach of his own, 'You do understand that we're all living in an experimental situation here, don't you?' he would say. 'This is one big sound laboratory.' Later he realized things were starting to get out of hand, but by then it was too late to cut off the power supply. It would have amounted to a declaration of war between him and the Busbar, resulting at the very least in broken windows every week and other inconveniences of that kind.

It was a fate that had already befallen Edelweiss. Once, in the very early days, the Busbar had asked the Edelweiss studios to supply it with electricity. The residents refused, which was a mistake as from that day onwards their windows were smashed with relentless regularity. You could no longer sit and relax outside the front door, since Edelweiss territory ended at the threshold, as would be made graphically clear to any unwary violator within a minute. Ever since the refusal, their front terrace had been permanently smeared with crap and puke. If one of the Busbar regulars needed to pee, he would walk outside and water the glass frontage of Edelweiss. This went on for months.

Sometimes there would be a brief truce. One of the young men at the Busbar might even start up a conversation. To a mother: 'Nice daughters you have.' She: 'The big one or the little one?' He, beer bottle in one hand as ever: 'Give me the little one.'

The most important source of sustenance and enjoyment for most of the island's residents was freely available, thanks to the liberal Dutch drugs policy. The main dealer was the firm Beer and Co., and the quantities delivered were beyond the bounds of anyone's imagination. At least once a week a large trailer appeared in front of the Busbar and hundreds of crates were unloaded. There were weeks in which the number of crates was in the thousands. The profits for the Busbar in those months must have been dizzying.

Other drugs were in circulation on the island too – a little heroin and cocaine, a lot of pills, sometimes a bit of hash – but they didn't cause anyone much trouble. Only when certain pills were used in combination with products of the firm Beer and Co. might difficulties arise. Suddenly someone would run out of a hut shouting 'Who's nicked my bread? Who's nicked my bread?' He'd start a fight with a random passer-by or attempt to set fire to his own home. The others would race over and try to calm things down, but sometimes the flames spread and one or other of the villages would experience a minor eruption of collective insanity and rage.

There was a distinct hierarchy among users of different pleasure-inducing substances. The alcoholics, for example, felt themselves vastly superior to the trippers. The junkies weren't even talked about; they were simply scum. Several huts were flattened by the alcoholics purely because heroin addicts lived in them.

Still, a daily intake of ten or fifteen half-litre bottles of Leeuw lager did not leave the human psyche entirely unscathed. In and around the Busbar there were sometimes dramatic scenes. 'I smashed his brains in,' one of the young men, by the name of Adriaan, roared one night. 'I cracked his skull. Blood! Blood!' He did indeed have a large brick in his hand, covered in blood, but it was probably from a chicken. Nowhere far or near could anyone find anything that looked the slightest bit like a skull fracture. Adriaan didn't last long at the Busbar. Even for the island people he was too wild.

In a physical sense too, the months-long consumption of beer had its effects. Priscilla, a girl of about twenty, developed an abscess on her thigh of almost mediaeval proportions. Only when it became unbearable did she visit the first-aid post, and she failed to show up for further appointments, preferring to sit by her fire smoking grass and drinking beer.

'Island sores', the residents called ulcers and swellings like that. Some people got them after only a few months, and they never went away. Many islanders walked around barefoot all day, rarely washed, and drank so much alcohol that their resistance quickly declined. 'Drink was the main problem on most of the island, far more so than drugs,' said Dr Leen van Trigt later. He held consultations month after month at the council first-aid post. To a provider of medical services like him, the island was one of the so-called 'finding places', where the most problematic of vagrants were to be found because there was something on offer, food, shelter, warmth.

The doctor's surgery was used mainly by foreigners – most of the Dutch had channels of their own – and more than half of them had skin diseases. Intestinal complaints were common as well, another consequence of extreme alcohol intake. There were remarkably few sexually transmitted diseases. Drink makes you impotent. Some of the girls made a living by prostitution, but they weren't a sex-crazed bunch, in fact a large proportion of the island's population was composed of ordinary couples living in harmony.

No, the island sores, the ulcers and swellings, they were the big problem. Even the residents themselves began to notice that odd and inexplicable things were happening. The slightest little cut might fester for weeks and hardly anything ever healed normally. People had their own explanation for that, one that fitted the philosophy of life that most of them, for all their differences, shared. They believed they were the true oppressed, society's casualties, the eternal victims of circumstances beyond their control. Where the island sores were concerned, their victimhood was obvious, it was the island that was causing the sores.

One girl believed the plague had begun when pigeons from Chernobyl arrived in Amsterdam. She said they'd started to moult on the island, scattering radioactive feathers and dust everywhere. A German woman found several skulls and bones – in reality dumped there as building land by a contractor after the digging out of an old chapel in the city centre – and she told everyone it was all because Hitler had ordered the Amsterdammers to sacrifice a hundred thousand Jews to him, otherwise he'd destroy the city the way he'd destroyed Rotterdam. The Amsterdammers had done so, she said, on this very island, hence the sores. But most of the residents had a more prosaic explanation, namely that the ground was full of chemicals, and they increasingly named a large oil company as the biggest culprit. As for the fact that in all those years no supplies other than timber, cocoa, tobacco and cotton had been unloaded on the island and the firm in question had never set foot there, well, arguments like that might count for something in town, but not on the island.

Now it has to be said that this way of thinking made for an extremely relaxed attitude to life. Most residents got up at around ten or eleven, maybe one. They wandered about for a bit, pulled a piece of plastic sheeting straight, sometimes ran a broom over their floor and then gathered around a fire, where each of them opened a bottle of beer. They threw a bit of wood into the flames, or something else, whatever happened to be within reach. Karel came along swearing on his one leg, Bicycle Repair Man told a story about a good fight, and so the day slipped by.

Sometimes there was something to do. One day a truck appeared on the terrain, ripe for demolition. Dozens went at it, like ants on a dying may bug. The front was secured, another truck was tied to the back and with a single tug the superstructure was wrenched off. Next came the dismantling. Everything of the slightest value was removed, wood, aluminium, copper. After two hours only the carcass was left.

Such a collective explosion of activity was the exception, however. In retrospect it's clear that life on the island was filled with what are known as 'intrinsic pursuits', activities undertaken purely for their own sake, not aimed at achieving anything else. Sauntering, standing still, having a drink and chatting are all acts of which the purpose is closely connected to the activity as such, indeed in which purpose and activity generally form an inextricable whole.

In the city such activities had lost virtually all significance. Almost everything was undertaken purely because it rendered up something else: money, fame, power, a more advantageous position. On the island, although elements of this were present, the tone was nevertheless set by a different rhythm: action for action's sake, living for living's sake.

Yet it was not enough, and the reason for that was the island itself. The island was a dead end. No one passed through on the way to somewhere else, nothing new happened by, and most acts arose from an impulse that sparked into life, spread illumination for ten minutes at best and then went out again. The terrain was full of the results, structures barely started, half-executed plans and global projects stillborn.

Fire was the only thing that drew people, and it was around fires that most of the residents sat, like French tramps in a black-and-white film from the 1950s. Aidy, Maff and Patrick of the Busbar were among the few who kept themselves busy with something constructive. In the wrecked 'office' on the roof of their Palace Flophouse they set up a computer and began to master the rudiments of bookkeeping.

Then, as if out of a sky rent asunder, Mutoid Waste descended on the island.

Suddenly, on a sunny June afternoon in the year 1989, there they were. Five or six large buses, a heavy-duty generator and a crane rode onto the island. They stopped behind one of the warehouses. Steps flapped down, generators started up, lamps came on and astonishing installations edged onto the terrain. Mutoid Waste's every act was carried out with the efficiency of an army in the field. The whole island came out to look. No one had ever seen anything like it. Such a pace, such good-quality materials, and everything worked!

The Mutoid Waste Company was a thirty-strong group that had already been travelling around Europe for about fifteen years, setting itself up at places where there was sufficient waste to hand, such as demolition sites, factories and major cities. On dumping grounds like the island they would find the building blocks for their art installations, all of which were intended to tell the story of the senselessness of our Western throwaway society.

The Mutoid Waste people were magicians. In two weeks they welded together everything in sight. They made a fence out of fused car wrecks. They rode around on a bicycle they'd built that was three metres high. They made huge butterflies and grasshoppers out of tubing and discarded plastic. Out at the coast, on top of the highest dune, they constructed a gigantic fist out of pipes and vats, amid the columns of smoke from the Hoogovens steelworks. They cut cars in half and put them together in their own eccentric combinations. They built a metres-high marionette out of auto parts and hung it from a gallows. And everywhere they mounted lights and gas pipes, so that at night everything flickered, shone or even spouted fire.

The island was flabbergasted. Compared to this, the Busbar was an old folks' club. No one dared say a word when the guys from Mutoid immediately appropriated one of the best spots. Electricity was no problem at all, it was provided without hesitation by Edelweiss. With their inconceivable energy they immediately bent everything to their will.

The island was badly in need of the people from Mutoid Waste. They could make stoves, weld tent frames, jack up caravans, repair cars and do a thousand other indispensable but almost forgotten jobs.

That was the way it had gone with Mutoid Waste all over Europe. They came, performed a few essential tasks, built the decor for a vast spectacle, earned a little money, and left. And that was how it went here as well. After three weeks the caravan moved on, towards Berlin I believe, and it was quiet again. Quieter than ever.

The terrain was now so full that the distinction between useful objects, such as wood, aluminium, plastic and bottles, less useful objects such as old dishcloths and almost empty jam jars, and completely useless trash, like used sanitary towels and food scraps more than a week old, grew increasingly vague.

The rubbish piled up. The mobile toilets provided by the city council were always blocked. For lack of toilet paper, people used Saturday supplements, old underpants, cloths and rags, so there was a permanent overflow. The tips Van den Berg had to slip the plumbers to get the whole lot working again were rising week by week.

Meanwhile, every Tuesday afternoon at the town hall, officials Bos, Mell, Aalders, Van den Berg, Van Stuyvenberg and

Blankenzee reviewed the state of affairs on KNSM Island item by item. The minutes of their meetings have been preserved for posterity. A few excerpts:

5 July 1989
– Blankenzee rustles up a fridge
– Occupation density: stable
– Trouble: Aalders reports a stabbing
– Notice board: has been ordered
– Festival: organizers are working on a permit application

18 July 1989
– Notice board: has been ordered and is nearly ready. Stewards will contact residents of Levantkade 6 about its placement

22 August 1989
– Notice board: residents of Levantkade refuse placement on their frontage; Blankenzee will have it erected on poles
– Shower: soap is rather expensive. Van den Berg will ask the health department about cheaper options
– Occupation density: the terrain is full

29 August 1989
– Festival: is now over, other than some dribs and drabs. Blankenzee and the stewards are assessing the damage
– Toilet block: same old trouble
– Notice board: is being erected, anti-graffiti coating will be applied if necessary

12 September 1989
– Occupation density: terrain is gradually emptying, partly because the atmosphere is worsening rapidly
– Notice board: will be erected at the end of next week

26 September 1989
– Occupation density: terrain is emptying. Several structures have been abandoned
– Notice board: erected and set on fire within 12 hours; Blankenzee will report the offence

The notice board had cost five thousand guilders. In all the tongues of Babylon it warned that the city was intending to build on the terrain shortly. And that camping was forbidden.

That summer saw one more big festival, organized by Aidy, Patrick, Sean, Maff, Jasin, Sil, Ludo and a few others. They had staged something similar on the island the year before, but this was to be the party to end all parties.

First of all, the lads at the Busbar put together a letter of invitation to bands and, even more importantly, to sponsors. 'Hi,' they wrote. 'To introduce & explain ourselves, we are all active, constructive people who used to travel the Festivals (Stonehenge etc.) but because of state & police attitudes were forced to venture abroad in search of a peaceful free festival atmosphere.' 'The aim of this festival', they wrote in their next stencil, 'is to give energy, enthusiasm and solidarity to all kindred spirits, the squatter movement, ecology, in short all those who care about life, liberty and the pursuit of happiness.'

With infectious enthusiasm, Aidy, Patrick, Maff and the

others then started on a massive task, the building of a large stage at the back of Edelweiss, around which tens of thousands of young people would be able to dance, celebrate and commune with each other.

Festival fever took over the rest of the island. Stalls were set up everywhere selling sandwiches, cakes and second-hand clothes. The bosses of the Busbar even went to the town hall in person. In heavy leathers, legs on the desk, they confronted a group of astonished officials and requested an official permit.

On the long-awaited weekend itself the rain bucketed down. Of all those thousands of 'kindred spirits', only a few hundred showed up. The bands refused to play in the downpours for fear of being electrocuted. Out of desperation the last few acts of the festival were moved to one of the warehouses.

Meanwhile the stage had acquired a different function. Even while the festival was still going on, the first couples moved into the big empty spaces under the platform, which soon became one of the most popular residential locations on the island.

So autumn began while it was still summer.

There had always been people on the island who kept their distance from the rest, and Jos, a Belgian labourer who had some kind of problem with the tax authorities in his homeland, was an example. He lived in a caravan not far from Edelweiss and didn't want anything to do with 'the claptrap those people talk'. 'I sit in the sun in front of my caravan and keep the curtains shut behind me. No problem at all.' Or Rick, who mostly stayed in the background but, as a former social worker, often assumed a crucial role in times of crisis. He was proud of always having stuck to his principles, no stealing, no drugs, not too much to drink. 'I've managed it pretty well up to now.' There were others like him.

There were also outsiders, people who even by the standards of the island did things that were just too crazy. No one minded that old Karel stepped out of his caravan in the mornings wearing his rat-chewed cap surrounded by the greenish brown stink of a hundred and fifty half-starved animals. Nor did anyone have any trouble with Ben, who walked along the water's edge all day, rocking, with a pair of ear protectors as headphones and a radio on his shoulder that hadn't made a sound in years. The same went for Alex and Maevis, who lived permanently under the spell of certain purple pills. One day they left for the city centre, having had a vision that behind the Central Station, in the IJ, lay a treasure chest 'full of old coins'. They couldn't stop telling each other about it.

Henry was a more difficult case. He came from England and no one knew much about him. He could stare out over the water for hours, and the doctor sometimes had to talk him down from a high embankment wall where he was getting on everyone's nerves. He said that with a final leap into the ice-cold, stormy IJ he wanted finally to prove that he was somebody, a person who dared to do what no one had ever done before. Later he was arrested for trying to set light to a large timber warehouse on the far outer edge of the city.

Then there was Tom, who always liked to go around naked and whose real name everyone had long forgotten, including Tom. Sometimes you might come across him in town. He'd be wearing swimming trunks and a snorkel, say, walking along the Kloveniersburgwal with a hand towel and suntan lotion, staring for minutes on end at the sand and the waves rolling in.

Tom wasn't always able to keep his hands off the children. Eventually he was ejected from the island as a result, but he managed to find a place to stay again later, in a friend's hut. He wasn't a guest there for long. One morning he was loudly ejected from his new housemate's shelter: 'You've done it again, you filthy swine. I saw you do it. You were fucking LeMond!' LeMond himself said nothing. He just stood there, surveying the scene, wagging his tail.

Finally there was Danny. Danny with the two faces. Danny was a child of the devil: he had the sweetest face in the world, yet he could beat a person half to death – and did so with great regularity. He was once chased off the island, but he walked back over the bridge again within an hour, with a look as innocent as a child's.

There was more and more fighting as that summer wore on. During the week it seemed as if most of the island's residents had office jobs in town, but every weekend they were at it again. There were fires, too, more and more unexplained fires. It became common for something 'simply' to catch fire, which was more frightening each time it happened.

One Saturday night Carly suddenly found herself sitting bolt upright in bed. It was one of those moments when she knew that something was seriously wrong. The air was filled with the shattering of glass, shouts and the sound of cars driving about. She recognized Danny's voice: 'I hate Germans, I hate Mercedes-Benzes, I hate Mercedes-Benzes,' and through the window she watched him trying to beat up the Cakebaker. A little later he was seen running around with fire and petrol, and one dumpster after another caught light. Before long a car and a caravan were on fire. He'd torched his own things. Soon after that came loud screaming from the toilet cubicles. Danny had thrown a molotov cocktail inside while one of the girls was relieving herself.

That was enough. Never before had the island asked the police to arrest someone. It went against the first, main, unwritten rule of the island: we take care of our own shit. Rick gestured to Carly, one of the few who had a phone. The Cakebaker and Patrick nodded. Police cars drove onto the island and not a further word was said. It was clear to even the most deranged residents that the survival of the island was at stake.

As the cops were about to put handcuffs on Danny they hesitated for a moment. 'Are we really sure this is the guilty party?' Danny had put on his angel face again.

After Black Sunday, as it became known, something like peace settled over the island again for a while. Relations between the lads at the Busbar and the squatters in Edelweiss improved. The time of threats, puke, piss and smashed windows was over. Territories had been clearly demarcated, and at the same time none of that really mattered so much any longer.

The final months passed slowly and calmly. The campfires went on burning and as the evenings drew in, the atmosphere became warm and intimate.

There was increasing talk about leaving. At the town hall, plans for the area had taken shape. In December building work would begin with the demolition of a number of old warehouses, and before then the island would have to be cleared. Men in new cars were spotted more and more often amid the caravans and shacks. They never stayed long. If someone walked up to them in a half-fantasy commando uniform, with a bandana on his head and a dagger in his belt, the architects and property developers would usually duck back behind the wheel as quickly as they could.

Yet somewhere an inexorable mechanism had started up and everyone could feel it, cogs and gears grinding towards all of them, junkies or alcoholics, the Busbar as well as Tripper Village. Apart from the elite, that is. The squatters in the studios would be allowed to stay. Artists do not get evicted.

Some people did indeed start to leave. Marloes had to give back her borrowed minibus and in early November she moved into an empty hole in the ground at the Devil's Bend with her three children and three dogs. They had a few sheets of corrugated asbestos to cover them. Rick occasionally took them a carrier bag of food, if he'd managed to earn something somewhere on the docks.

Other empty huts were taken over in those final months by a new, strange kind of resident, shadowy figures from Columbia, Moroccan boys who lived by pick-pocketing and bag-snatching.

Council workers arrived on the terrain bearing incomprehensible missives. 'To take action to end your residence on or occupation of the terrain in question, which is in violation of several local ordinances...' 'In violation of article 10 of the regulations governing mobile homes...' 'In violation of article 47 paragraph 1 and article 55 of the housing act in conjunction with 345/348 of the building code...'

The steward called Bos, an alderman's right hand man, decided to deliver the 'notice of an administrative order' in person. He managed to pass a few copies to a group of complicatedly dressed girls, but most of the letters were thrown into the fires unread. At the Busbar his mission came to a premature end when the box full of enforcement orders was walloped out of his hands with a well-aimed karate blow. Bos left, and his article 47 paragraph 1 and article 55 of the housing act in conjunction with 345/348 of the building code fluttered down a hundredfold onto the ground around Edelweiss.

The islanders meanwhile were making increasingly attractive plans of their own, Italy, Berlin, Portugal. But there was always something – a broken exhaust, a friend to wait for, unhelpful weather.

Some did leave in the end. And sure enough the odd colourful postcard arrived, showing beaches and blue skies and bearing authentic Italian stamps. Others left for as yet unclaimed stretches of the banks of the IJ a few kilometres away, which they had 'scouted out' several months earlier, 'just in case'.

One day a Mercedes drove onto the terrain and stopped at the German Triangle. One of the girls emerged and a mother and father got out of the car, beaming, belongings were loaded into the boot and off the family went, homewards, over the bridge, to start a new life in the safety of Bavaria.

Sometimes those who remained said to each other: 'The longer you stay here, the more chance you have of ending up dead.' Because the threat of eviction wasn't all. The sores were spreading across the island like the plague. For months now, anyone who so much as ran their nails over their skin had a chance of contracting an infection, and the tiniest scratch became an ulcer that never healed.

During that time, Leen van Trigt saw a girl at his surgery

that he happened to have watched arrive a few months before. She looked quite different now. 'I still used to wash at first,' she confided to him in a burst of candour. 'But everything is such chaos now that I prefer to stay in bed all day.'

The island had become a swamp.

Then the first demolition men showed up. They started with the roof of one of the warehouses across from Edelweiss. Their pounding and hammering echoed terrifyingly across the terrain.

One night a man drove onto the island. It seems he was intending to dump his car in the IJ – he must have had a good reason – but somehow something went magically wrong. The next morning the residents saw a large, shiny car hanging above the water a few meters out from the edge, like a kebab with a mooring post as a skewer. Still, after all those months nothing could surprise them.

At the far end of the Noordzeeweg, beyond even the Radarweg and the Turbineweg, where you almost fall off the edge of the city and the world consists purely of weeds, scrap timber, Hazardous Substances and wrecked cars, lives Willem Gouw, better known as Willem the Burner. He's a demolition man and his face resembles a Romanian landscape, covered in mountains, valleys, rivers and streams, like life itself. Along with his wife Anna and his daughter Sandra he lives in barracks between the corrugated warehouses and heaped up Toyotas and Chevrolets.

It's quiet and lonely on that strange boundary between city and countryside. You come upon foxes, hares, rabbits, owls and pheasants. Here and there, hidden amid the scrap metal, lurk feral pets from the city. Sandra lives there in her own world, has her own places and her own bits of land. 'That's my hobby,' she says. She can make ladybirds, she puts four in a jar and after a week there are eight. She can do that. The area is called the Heining, a bit of the city once famous as the place where a brewer was held by his kidnappers, although everyone immediately forgot about that once it was over. Willem burns rubbish and trades in this and that. Near him are a fertilizer business, a firewood dealership, a large timber store, another demolition man, Jan Lor, and beyond them another stretch of land that no one has used for a while.

One cold, rainy day in November all that changed. Men from the Heidemaatschappij appeared and started paving the area with concrete slabs. Less than twenty-four hours later the silence was suddenly broken by a procession on a grand scale: tow trucks, police vans, motorcycle cops, and a long line of low-loaders carrying the most remarkable collection of caravans, buses and camper vans that Willem the Burner had seen in his long career. Some had people sitting in them. One featured rats crawling up the insides of the windows and a wildly gesturing man walking nearby, a kind of one-legged Rasputin with a goatee beard and a hood like a monk. There was an old bus containing a couple of men with tattoos and leather jackets who kept shouting, and a mother with three bouviers and three children. It was an unreal and very long movie scene.

The men of the Heidemaatschappij were as surprised as anyone. They hadn't been expecting the procession for another week and half, the terrain was still one great quagmire. There were no toilet trailers as yet, no running water, and it was an hour's walk to the nearest shop. The Heining was a storage depot, so the buses and caravans were packed in next to each other, often with less than twenty centimetres between them – not enough for a pivoting window to open. The only problem for the city was that they were all still inhabited.

In the end the clearance of the island had come like a bolt from the blue. One night, a week earlier, pink and yellow light had suddenly flared over the island. The old customs warehouse was ablaze and figures could be seen running back and forth to the studios to save what they could. Firemen were searching for hydrants – in vain, since they were buried under the huts, mounds of rubbish and slabs of concrete.

The fire was not unexpected. One of the stewards, Van den Berg, had warned his colleagues several days before that 'there would be trouble' if the demolition went ahead, and that at the very least they could expect 'all kinds of hot-headed behaviour'. And hadn't some of the guys at the Busbar said that when everyone was evicted from the island, they were going to 'lay on the biggest barbecue in Holland'? Everyone asked what had got into the city to make it decide to start demolition work before the evictions took place. After all, everything was well ahead of schedule.

When the demolition men left that Friday evening without even taking the trouble to slide shut the doors to the warehouses they were working on, it was generally seen as an invitation. 'A sort of rank hysteria hung over the island,' one of the residents of Edelweiss would say later. 'Everyone felt something was coming. They'd been talking about it under their breath for weeks. The apathy and craziness finally flipped over into collective insanity.' Then the first customs warehouse really did burn down.

The fire was high and fierce. It quickly spread to one of the artists' buildings. Six studios were completely burnt out and another fourteen were damaged. The next morning the residents stood and wept as they surveyed the wreckage. Friends were hurriedly called in to help and they tried to save what they could. Six artists had lost all their work, which in many cases had taken them years to create. Fourteen others found most of it ruined, grey and covered in a kind of liquid soot.

Then the looting began.

The guys from the Busbar ran up, laughing and joking. Wherever they saw the chance they pulled everything of value to them out of the half-empty studios: zinc, lead, copper. Bronze artworks were stolen, other work smashed.

In the days that followed, everything threatened to get out of hand. Officially the eviction wasn't due for another two weeks, but the squatters of Edelweiss were terrified that they'd be the arsonists' next target. Beneath the pillars supporting the building were piles of wood and other leftovers from the Junkie Village. If a fire broke out there, Edelweiss would become a vast glowing oven in no time.

Meanwhile the old war of nerves between the established residents and outsiders had broken out again, as intense as ever. Patrick threatened daily, 'You don't like fire, you gonna lose, we gonna burn you down.' It was clear that Edelweiss had it coming, the entire Busbar was determined about that.

In the strictest confidence, the police told some of the squatters over the next few days that the eviction would take place a week earlier than announced, to avoid giving the Busbar a chance to set fire to everything systematically.

That Friday, at half past seven in the morning, Rick caught bus 28 into town. He had a job to do there. On the way he saw long lines of riot squad vans, tow trucks and low loaders. He didn't pay any attention, mainly because he thought it had something to do with the ceremonial entry of Sinta Klaas into town, or something like that. It wasn't until nine-thirty that he heard they'd been clearing KNSM Island for an hour already. By the time he rushed back it was too late. He'd missed the chance to fetch his valuables out of his caravan: a few photos, a portable television... All he managed to get was the address of the Heining.

When the eviction started, there were several arrests. The lads at the German Triangle, who had never caused any trouble on the island, turned out to be notorious in town as fences and queer-bashers. The boyfriend of the girl who'd been taken back to Bavaria by contented parents a few weeks earlier was suspected of robbing and murdering two elderly people, one in Delft and another in Het Gooi.

Even before the riot squad arrived, the staff of the Busbar began pouring everybody generous measures of whisky. They were so outnumbered that at first nothing happened, but anyone who knew Andy, Sean, Jason, Maff and Patrick knew they were not going to take this lying down.

While the first caravans were being loaded onto trailers, the riot police felt they could allow themselves a moment's respite. They withdrew to the bridge. By the time they'd left the terrain, Tripper Village was ablaze. The firemen had no sooner arrived than the big old stage caught light. A few minutes later the first of the containers went up in flames.

It was the start of a miserable few hours. Everyone was thrown off the island, immediately, with no by your leave. The Busbar was cleared out, but so were dozens of tents, huts and hovels belonging to the many residents who had never hurt a fly and were simply scratching out an existence for themselves in their own way. Bulldozers flattened the shiny wigwam, Willem's house with its skylight and mosaics, the circus family's garden, the Cakebaker's shop, James' luxury hut and the butterflies built by Mutoid Waste – it was all bulldozed and shovelled together, leaving nothing but three rubbish dumps, three great heaps of old clothes, wood, plastic sheeting, food scraps, bicycles, chairs, mattresses, blankets, sofas, pans, bottles, tin cans, plastic bags, car parts, grey-greenish and rust-brown, all that was left of a year and a half of living and working on the island.

How things went with most of the island's residents after that I don't know.

Willem, the man with the mosaic house, was last heard of heading south, towards the sun and the blue postcards. Carly still lives above Edelweiss.

A few of the illegals moved to Leefland, a lonely stretch of grass and shrubs amid oil storage tanks, not far from the Heining. The group around the Busbar settled on an abandoned terrain near the old Houthaven, where timber was once landed. Several of those left behind by Mutoid Waste moved into a squat called De Wielingen in the south of the city and after that disappeared.

Marloes, with her dogs and her children, became caught in a vicious circle of hunger and isolation. More and more often the whole lot of them were too weak to make the long cycle trip, against the wind, from the Heining to Hare Krishna, Mother Theresa, the Sisters of Mercy, the market and the city's other crumb-tables. She later moved to the centre of town with her children, to one squat after another, eternally fleeing her ex-husband, the Powerful, Important Man who, with his thousands of Connections, held the world in his grip like an octopus.

Jos lived on the Heining for months. He was in charge of the first-aid post there.

Karel the rat king got sick. His neighbours saw him cycling away with his one leg, down the long road to the station, lurching forwards again and again with one great angry thrust of the pedals. He was from a small town in South Holland and he disappeared into a hospital there. The young man left to care for Karel's army of rats inevitably neglected them, so that after two weeks only a few dozen were left, feeding on the remains of their kin. In the end the caravan and all it contained was hauled to Karel's home town by Willem the Burner, Jos the Belgian and the writer of these lines, where it was left outside the door of the town hall, the last of the rats still jumping up against the taped-shut windows.

New, strange inhabitants moved onto the Heining, men with expensive cars and smart clothes. The Moroccan lads arrived too, more now than ever, and at weekends the evenings and nights were full of the coming and going of upmarket vehicles.

After a few months, with a little help from Thijs van den Berg, Rick was able to drag his caravan into the courtyard of a large squat, but there he became so sick he could hardly move. Sometimes Marloes would bring him a plastic bag with a little food in it. No one else cared about him in the slightest.

When the summer ended, I lost track even of them.

Bij de productie van dit boek is gebruikgemaakt van papier dat het keurmerk Forest Stewardship Council® (FSC®) draagt. Bij dit papier is het zeker dat de productie niet tot bosvernietiging heeft geleid. Ook is het papier 100% chloor- en zwavelvrij gebleekt.

FSC
www.fsc.org
MIX
Papier van
verantwoorde herkomst
FSC® C110751